Japan's Effectiveness as a Geo-economic Actor:
Navigating Great-power Competition

Yuka Koshino

Robert Ward

'This book is essential reading for anyone seeking to understand Japan's national-security policy. With China's emergence
as a major challenger to the liberal international order, Tokyo's
recent leaders have taken new steps to defend Japan's advanced
technologies, critical infrastructure and supply chains, as well
as to use its technological advantages to strengthen its national
security for the first time since 1945. Nothing could be a better
introduction to this essential topic than this superbly written
book by these IISS experts in Japanese policy.'

*– Kanehara Nobukatsu, Professor of Doshisha University in Kyoto; former assis-
tant chief cabinet secretary to prime minister Abe Shinzo and inaugural deputy
secretary-general of Japan's National Security Secretariat*

Japan's Effectiveness as a Geo-economic Actor:
Navigating Great-power Competition

Yuka Koshino

Robert Ward

IISS The International Institute for Strategic Studies

The International Institute for Strategic Studies

Arundel House | 6 Temple Place | London | WC2R 2PG | UK

First published March 2022 by **Routledge**
4 Park Square, Milton Park, Abingdon, Oxon, OX14 4RN

for **The International Institute for Strategic Studies**
Arundel House, 6 Temple Place, London, WC2R 2PG, UK
www.iiss.org

Simultaneously published in the USA and Canada by **Routledge**
52 Vanderbilt Avenue, New York, NY 10017

Routledge is an imprint of Taylor & Francis, an Informa Business

© 2022 The International Institute for Strategic Studies

The International Institute for Strategic Studies is an independent centre for research, information and debate on the problems of conflict, however caused, that have, or potentially have, an important military content. The Council and Staff of the Institute are international and its membership is drawn from almost 100 countries. The Institute is independent and it alone decides what activities to conduct. It owes no allegiance to any government, any group of governments or any political or other organisation. The IISS stresses rigorous research with a forward-looking policy orientation and places particular emphasis on bringing new perspectives to the strategic debate.

The Institute's publications are designed to meet the needs of a wider audience than its own membership and are available on subscription, by mail order and in good bookshops. Further details at www.iiss.org.

British Library Cataloguing in Publication Data
A catalogue record for this book is available from the British Library

Library of Congress Cataloging in Publication Data

ADELPHI series
ISSN 1944-5571

ADELPHI 481–483
ISBN 978-1-032-32139-4

Contents

AUTHORS

Yuka Koshino is a Research Fellow for Security and Technology Policy at the International Institute for Strategic Studies (IISS), conducting independent research on security in the Indo-Pacific region and the impact of emerging technologies on security from defence and geo-economic perspectives. She was previously affiliated with the Asia-Pacific Initiative in Tokyo as the inaugural Matsumoto–Samata Fellow (2020–21). Prior to joining the IISS, she served as a research associate with the Japan Chair at the Center for Strategic and International Studies. She holds a master's in Asian Studies from the Edmund A. Walsh School of Foreign Service at Georgetown University and a BA in Law from Keio University, where she completed an academic year at the University of California, Berkeley.

Robert Ward holds the Japan Chair at the International Institute for Strategic Studies (IISS), conducting independent research and writing extensively on strategic issues related to Japan. He is also the IISS Director of Geo-economics and Strategy, focusing on a range of issues including global economic governance, rules and standards setting, and how economic coercion affects policy at a national and corporate level. Prior to joining the IISS, he was Editorial Director at the Economist Intelligence Unit. Robert lived and worked in Japan from 1989 to 1996, latterly holding a position in Japan's largest credit-rating agency, the Japan Bond Research Institute. Robert holds bachelor's and master's degrees from Cambridge University.

ACKNOWLEDGEMENTS

This *Adelphi* book represents some of the conclusions reached during research undertaken by the authors in the first two years of the IISS Japan Chair Programme. The programme was made possible by a generous endowment from the Government of Japan in 2019. Its mission is to undertake independent research on Japan's security and foreign policies.

In conceptualising and writing this book, we were fortunate in being able to draw on a range of experts both inside and outside the Institute, whose comments and advice improved and tightened our arguments.

In the case of the former, we owe a particular debt of gratitude to Bill Emmott, Chair of the IISS Trustees; Tim Huxley, the former Executive Director of IISS–Asia; and Benjamin Rhode, Editor of the *Adelphi* series, who edited, advised and restructured the book, and were generous with their time and specialist advice. We are also grateful to IISS colleagues Nigel Inkster, James Crabtee, Dana Allin, Nigel Gould-Davies and David Gordon for their help in shaping this volume in our internal *Adelphi* 'struggle session'.

In the case of the latter, we were fortunate to be able to interview a number of policy specialists and practitioners from Japan, including Dr Funabashi Yoichi, Chairman and Founder of the Asia Pacific Initiative (API) in Tokyo; Kanehara Nobukatsu, former Assistant Chief Cabinet Secretary and inaugural Deputy Secretary–General of the National Security Secretariat of Japan in the second administration of Abe Shinzo; and Terazawa Tatsuya, former Vice Minister of the Ministry of Economy, Trade and Industry and Special Advisor to the Cabinet Office on economic security. Others, however, have preferred to remain anonymous.

We are also grateful to Dr Funabashi for the API Matsumoto–Samata Fellowship, a two-year programme that sends Japanese researchers at the start of their careers to foreign think tanks in order to nurture the next generation of leaders. Yuka Koshino was the first Matsumoto–Samata Research Fellow.

We would like to thank the Institute's formidable team of subeditors, designers and proof-readers who made much-appreciated improvements to the book's flow and voice.

Finally, we would like to thank our families for their support and forbearance during the writing of this book.

GLOSSARY

ATLA	Japan, Acquisition, Technology & Logistics Agency
ADIZ	Air Defence Identification Zone
ASDF	Japan, Air Self-Defense Force
API	Asia Pacific Initiative
AI	artificial intelligence
ARF	ASEAN Regional Forum
APEC	Asia-Pacific Economic Cooperation
ADB	Asian Development Bank
AIIB	Asian Infrastructure Investment Bank
AMF	Asian Monetary Fund
ASEAN	Association of Southeast Asian Nations
BAT	Baidu, Alibaba and Tencent
BMD	ballistic-missile defence
BOJ	Bank of Japan
BRI	Belt and Road Initiative
CMI	Chiang Mai Initiative
CMIM	Chiang Mai Initiative Multilateralization
CCP	Chinese Communist Party
CPTPP	Comprehensive and Progressive Agreement for Trans-Pacific Partnership
CoCom	Coordinating Committee for Multilateral Export Control
CST	Japan, Council for Science and Technology
CSTI	Japan, Council for Science, Technology and Innovation
CFEP	Japan, Council on Fiscal and Economic Policy
DFFT	Data Free Flow with Trust
DPJ	Democratic Party of Japan
DSSL	Designated State Secrets Law
DAG	Development Assistance Group

DSR	Digital Silk Road
EVSL	early voluntary sector liberalisation
EPA	Economic Partnership Agreement
EV	electric vehicle
FSA	Japan, Financial Services Agency
FOIP	Free and Open Indo-Pacific
FTA	free-trade agreement
GATT	General Agreement on Tariffs and Trade
GSOMIA	General Security of Military Information
GAFA	Google, Apple, Facebook and Amazon
GSDF	Japan, Ground Self-Defense Force
G7	Group of Seven
ICT	information and communications technology
IT	information technology
IMF	International Monetary Fund
ITU	International Telecommunication Union
JAXA	Japan Aerospace Exploration Agency
JBIC	Japan Bank of International Cooperation
JICA	Japan International Cooperation Agency
LDP	Japan, Liberal Democratic Party
MSDF	Japan, Maritime Self-Defense Force
MTDP	Japan, Medium Term Defense Program
SEAMCED	Ministerial Conference for the Economic Development of Southeast Asia
MOD	Japan, Ministry of Defense
METI	Japan, Ministry of Economy, Trade and Industry
MEXT	Japan, Ministry of Education, Culture, Sports, Science and Technology
MOFA	Japan, Ministry of Foreign Affairs

MIC	Japan, Ministry of Internal Affairs and Communications
MITI	Japan, Ministry of International Trade and Industry
MLIT	Japan, Ministry of Land, Infrastructure, Transport and Tourism
NSC	Japan, National Security Council
NSS	Japan, National Security Secretariat
NAFTA	North Atlantic Free Trade Agreement
ODA	official development assistance
OECD	Organisation for Economic Co-operation and Development
OPEC	Organization of the Petroleum Exporting Countries
PECC	Pacific Economic Cooperation Council
PKO	peacekeeping operation
PLA	China, People's Liberation Army
QII	Quality Infrastructure Investment
QKD	quantum key distribution
RAN	Radio Access Network
RCEP	Regional Comprehensive Economic Partnership
R&D	research and development
SCJ	Science Council of Japan
SLOC	sea line of communication
SC	Japan, Security Council
SDF	Japan, Self-Defense Forces
SMIC	Semiconductor Manufacturing International Corporation
SME	small and medium-sized enterprise
SEATO	Southeast Asia Treaty Organization
SSA	space situational awareness
TICAD	Tokyo International Conference on African Development
TPP	Trans-Pacific Partnership
VER	Voluntary Export Restraint
WTO	World Trade Organization

Introduction

Geo-economic strategy is not new: deploying economic instruments to secure foreign-policy aims and to project power has long been a core part of many countries' statecraft even before the advent of the term itself.[1] Analysts, meanwhile, have often sought to explain the link between economics and power. Writing in 1938, philosopher Bertrand Russell called economics an element in the 'science of power'.[2] In his seminal 1945 study of Germany's use of trade policy in the run-up to the Second World War, *National Power and the Structure of Foreign Trade*, Albert O. Hirschman wrote of how 'foreign economic relations can be used … as an instrument of national power policy'.[3] Writing in the 1970s, political scientist Joseph S. Nye spoke of 'the two-edged sword' nature of economic interdependence in international relations, citing the 'economic aspect' of national security.[4] In his 1987 study, *The Rise and Fall of the Great Powers*, historian Paul Kennedy, analysing imperial overstretch and the economic limits to national power, wrote: 'all of the major shifts in the world's *military-power* balances have followed alterations in the *productive* balances … where victory has always gone to the side with the greatest material resources.'[5]

The practice of geo-economics has an inseparable relationship with what might be termed 'economic security' – the safeguarding of national economic prosperity. Without a thriving national economy that is resilient to potential hostile measures by international adversaries, no state can use economic power effectively in order to achieve its geopolitical goals.

In 1990, as the Cold War ended, the historian Edward N. Luttwak provided the urtext of modern geo-economics, coining the term in his piece in the magazine *The National Interest*, 'From Geopolitics to Geo-Economics: Logic of Conflict, Grammar of Commerce', in which he assumed a 'steadily reducing importance of military power in world affairs' as 'states … reorient themselves toward geo-economics in order to compensate for their decaying geopolitical roles'.[6] The end of the Cold War in 1990, which coincided with the peak of Japan's extraordinary post-Second World War economic rise, appeared indeed to have 'ushered in a new era of geo-economics'.[7]

Concern about the link between economics and national power waned, however, during the 1990s.[8] In part this reflected the United States' emergence as the apparently unchallenged superpower and the benign growth environment for much of the rich world, which together bred complacency regarding the relationship between economics and security. The economic interdependence that followed the take-off of globalisation in the 1990s was seen in the West as an agent for promoting not just economic growth, but also liberal economic and political values. This was reinforced by the global economic boom that followed China's entry into the World Trade Organization (WTO) in 2001 and which lasted until the global financial crisis of 2008. In June 2001, on the eve of China's joining the WTO, *The Economist* newspaper forecasted that membership would 'bind China to international rules that will further diminish the role of government in the economy', citing those 'more optimistic

Chinese intellectuals [that] believe that economic globalisation will, over time, transform China politically as well'.[9]

Interest in geo-economics, however, has returned with a vengeance since the global financial crisis of 2007–08. China's rise has been less benign than disruptive for the West. Beijing has developed its 'own theory of "exceptionalism" to define its external engagement', thereby upsetting the global balance of power.[10] Moreover, China is a geo-economic power. As the world's second-largest economy and with a 1.4 billion-strong continental-sized domestic market, Beijing boasts significant geo-economic endowments, which it deploys to project Chinese power onto its neighbourhood and beyond. It does this through a mixture of economic inducements and coercion. A good example of the former is its multi-billion-US-dollar global development programme, the Belt and Road Initiative (BRI), while the latter is exemplified in the country denying access to its vast domestic markets to interlocutors that fail to toe Beijing's line on certain policy issues. Australia, Japan, Lithuania, the Philippines, South Korea and Taiwan have all been on the receiving end of Chinese economic coercion since 2010.

The economic interdependence fostered by globalisation and the resulting central position of China in the world's supply chains have strengthened Beijing's geo-economic hand. A study from McKinsey Global Institute in 2019 found that China was embedded in the global value chains of the highly traded electronics, machinery and equipment sectors, accounting for 17–28% of global exports of these goods, 9–16% of global imports and 38–42% of total output.[11] 'Manipulating the asymmetries of interdependence' is thus a key means by which Beijing wields power internationally.[12] This has opened new avenues for Chinese statecraft to challenge economic 'rules, norms, standards and protocols', which as one observer notes 'is where the Great Game of geo-economics is at play'.[13]

Geo-economic strategy may be an eternal feature of inter-national affairs, but its character thus evolves alongside the changing nature of the international economic system and the relative economic interdependence of its major powers. Those concerned with geo-economics, and economic security, are no longer primarily preoccupied with natural resources and terri-tory, but also with international supply chains, leading-edge technologies and their associated standards, as well as with the interaction between the civilian and military sectors frequently driving innovation.

China's rise and its propelling of geo-economics to the centre stage of contemporary international relations raises issues for all countries subscribing to the liberal international order, but perhaps particularly so for Japan. From the 1980s, Japanese offi-cial development assistance (ODA) and direct investment by Japanese companies helped to lay the foundations for China's economic modernisation, with Japan overwhelmingly having had the upper hand over China in terms of economic size and sophistication. But China's rise has transformed the dynamics of the bilateral relationship. By many measures, China is now Japan's most important economic partner. In 2002, China over-took the US as Japan's biggest source of imports and, by 2009, as its largest export market. China's demand for Japanese goods to fuel its rapid growth after WTO accession undoubtedly accelerated Japan's economic recovery after the bursting of its asset-price bubble in the early 1990s. Japanese firms have also been major investors in China, particularly since the 2007–08 financial crisis. Before the coronavirus pandemic started in 2020, China was also Japan's largest source of inbound tour-ists, accounting for one-third of the total during 2019. This drove the growth of Japan's domestic tourism sector, one of the success stories of then-prime minister Abe Shinzo's economic reforms, providing significant economic stimulus to Japan's

Figure 1: **Japanese and Chinese GDP compared, 1960–2020**

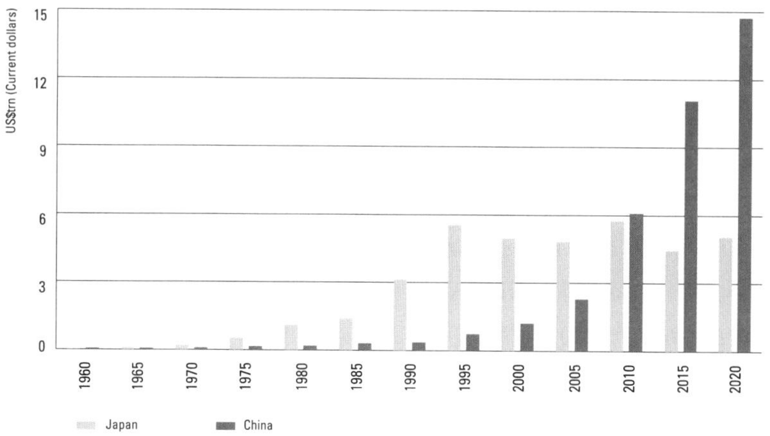

Source: World Bank database   ©IISS

cities and prefectures.[14] Although China still needs access to both Japanese technology and management know-how to raise the value added by its industry, Japan's economic relationship with China has become asymmetric. An important implication of this is that Tokyo cannot easily afford to antagonise Beijing and risk losing access to China's vast market and resources.

China also presents Japan with its most acute security challenges. Beijing has been outspending Tokyo on defence and out-investing Japan in emerging technologies, such as artificial intelligence (AI) and quantum computing, that have military as well as civil applications. In 2000, the defence budgets of China and Japan were of broadly similar size; by 2020, China's defence budget was four times larger than that of Japan. Beijing's spending on research and development (R&D) rose by a factor of ten from 2000 to 2017, while Japan's failed to even double.[15] The Japanese government now also frequently accuses China of 'revisionism', which it says is displayed in Beijing's 'unilateral attempts to change the status quo' in the region.[16] China's extensive territorial claims in the South China

Sea on the basis of its 'nine-dash line' demarcation and its construction of artificial islands there, both of which infringe international law, are examples of this.[17] There are grounds for believing that Beijing has defined the South China Sea as a national 'core interest', meaning that it will not negotiate its claims and may use force to defend them.[18] The South China Sea – as well as the closer East China Sea – are of particular concern to Tokyo given Japan's economic reliance on long sea lines of communication (SLOCs) that traverse both seas, sustaining its large resource needs and carrying its exports. Tokyo's and Beijing's SLOCs overlap in the South China Sea, and indeed elsewhere, making Beijing's territorial claims in the South China Sea a direct economic and security concern for Japan.[19] Beijing's increasing shrillness regarding its intention to absorb Taiwan serves only to further fuel Tokyo's strategic anxiety.

Japan's 'strange existence'

The rising importance of geo-economics in international relations should play to Japan's strengths. Economically, it has long been a giant. Accelerated by factors including the Korean War (which catalysed Japanese export growth), the '"Great Leap Forward" of the capitalist world economy' during the 1950s and 1960s, and by favourable national demography resulting from a post-Second World War baby boom, by the 1960s Japan already had the status of a 'great power' in economic terms.[20] By the early 1970s Japan had overtaken France, West Germany and the United Kingdom to become the world's second-largest economy.[21] Given the economic trauma and stagnation of the 1990s after the bursting of Japan's economic bubble – the largest asset-price collapse of the twentieth century – and the strengthening headwind of an ageing and then-shrinking domestic population, it was not surprising that in 2010 Japan's economy was overtaken by the rapidly growing Chinese economy for the global number-two position.[22] Although faster-growing and more populous emerging markets in the region such as India and Indonesia are now closing the gap in size with Japan's mature economy, it will remain in the top economic tier for several decades in terms of both its absolute size and the wealth of its market. Its economy will also remain larger than that of any other Western country, apart from the United States, into the second half of this century.[23]

Japan's size has made it an important global economic actor. A founding member of the Group of Seven (G7) group of industrialised economies in 1975, it has also long been the world's largest creditor and, after the US, a leading contributor to the Bretton Woods institutions.[24] Despite China's GDP having overtaken Japan's in 2010, the latter remains the second-largest financial contributor to the IMF and the World Bank Group, the third-largest to the UN, and, along with the US, the largest to the Asian Development Bank (ADB).[25] It is also one of the largest providers in cash terms of ODA, which is dispersed via the state development agency, the Japan International Cooperation Agency (JICA), and the state policy bank, the Japan Bank of International Cooperation (JBIC).[26] Japan is the largest sponsor of infra-structure projects in Southeast Asia despite China's efforts to expand its presence in the region through the BRI.[27] As of mid-2021, Japan's stock of investment in uncompleted projects in Indonesia, Malaysia, the Philippines, Thailand and Vietnam stood at US$259bn, compared with China's at US$157bn.[28] Japanese banks lend more to Southeast Asia's five largest economies (Indonesia, Malaysia, the Philippines, Thailand and Vietnam) than those of France, the UK and the US combined. Japan also remains one of the world's largest portfolio investors.[29]

Despite its economic size and influence, Japan's ability to exercise military statecraft – and therefore hard power – is constrained. This deprives it of the full spectrum of tools with which to project national power, giving rise to what Kosaka Masataka, one of Japan's leading post-Second World War international-relations thinkers, called Japan's 'strange existence' on the world stage.[30] This is partly the result of deliberate policy. Japan's constitution, promulgated in 1947 and now the world's oldest unamended such document, was drawn up against the backdrop of Japan's catastrophic defeat in the Second World War and the victorious Allies' desire to block any re-emergence of Japanese militarism. The preamble to the constitution pledges that 'never again shall [Japan] be visited with the horrors of war through the action of government', and Article 9 of the document states that 'the Japanese people forever renounce war as a sovereign right of the nation and the threat or use of force as means of settling international disputes'.[31] One lingering result of this has been the long-term conceptualisation of Japanese security thinking around an 'exclusively defence-oriented policy' (senshū bōei), meaning that 'defensive force is used only in the event of an attack'.[32] This has left a number of defence anomalies for Japan. Although by political convention Japan only spends around 1% of its GDP on defence, its large economy means that the absolute size of its defence budget is still considerable and was the world's eighth largest in 2020.[33] The constitution's provision that 'land, sea, and air forces, as well as other war potential, will never be maintained' means that for some observers the Self-Defense Forces (SDF, Japan's de facto armed forces) occupy a constitutional grey zone, or are 'simply unconstitutional'.[34] Japan therefore lacks a clearly delineated and agreed constitutional basis for ensuring its national security against external threats.

Given its parallel history of twentieth-century militarism, Germany is the main comparator for Japan's security predicament. The German constitution, however, puts no limits similar to Japan's on maintaining war potential, although Article 87a stipulates that the Federal Republic's armed forces are 'for [the] purposes of defence'.[35] In 2005, Germany also introduced a law to both allow and regulate the deployment of armed forces abroad.[36] Germany's membership of NATO is a further differentiator from Japan. As noted in a IISS *Adelphi* book on German security policy published in 2021, during the Cold War the German armed forces were 'optimised for collective defence within NATO, which, due to Germany's geographical position, was equivalent to territorial defence'.[37] At the end of the Cold War in 1990, Germany had more combat battalions in active service than either the UK or France. In contrast, Japan counts the US as its only formal security ally under the terms of the 1951 Japan–US Security Treaty.[38] There is, of course, no NATO equivalent in Asia, reflecting the United States' post-Second World War preference for a 'hub-and-spokes' system of bilateral alliances in the region that gave the US 'more leverage, while depriving allies of other rule makers or mediators'.[39] The closest equivalent in the region, the Southeast Asia Treaty Organization (SEATO), was disbanded in 1977 just over 22 years after its founding, having displayed neither 'a viable political purpose, [n]or a military function'.[40]

Yoshida Shigeru, the pivotal prime minister of Japan's early post-Second World War years who was in office in 1946–47 and 1948–54, built on the 'peace constitution' with what later became known as the Yoshida Doctrine.[41] This doctrine had three pillars: Japan was to rely militarily on the US, while maintaining a 'low posture' in global affairs and an 'economics above all' domestic policy stance that focused on domestic growth and foreign trade, and while spending minimally on armaments. Yoshida did not rule out the possibility of Japan eventually rearming and regaining its status as an independent military power.[42] But the immediate priority was the need for economic growth to heal the pressing post-Second World War divisions in Japan.[43] This 'low posture' stance, or 'passive internationalism', guided Japanese policy for much of the Cold War.[44] For most of this period, Japanese economic statecraft was often deployed with one eye on buttressing Japan's security alliance with the US amid frequent bouts of bilateral trade friction. There were also US voices who accused Japan of being a reactive and mercantile free-rider of the international order.

During the Cold War, the main challenge to the Yoshida Doctrine came from the Liberal Democratic Party (LDP) prime minister Nakasone Yasuhiro, who held office from 1982–87. Nakasone wanted to turn Japan into an 'international state' (*kokusai kokka Nihon e zenshin*) and a world technology leader, which would help propel Japan's broader global ambitions.[45] He also sought to bind Japan more closely into the security alliance with the US in order to counter the Soviet threat by agitating for Japan's 'autonomous defence' (*jishu bōei ron*). An early example of this was his cabinet's approval in January 1983 – just before Nakasone's visit to Washington that month – of the transfer of purely military technology to the US, and only to the US.[46] This was a significant tweak to the ban on exports of arms and military technology introduced in 1967 under prime minister Sato Eisaku (in office from 1964–72) and tightened in 1976 under prime minister Miki Takeo (in office 1974–76), and was intended to boost US–Japan security-alliance inter-operability. In 1986, Tokyo approved Japan's participation in US president Ronald Reagan's Strategic Defense Initiative – dubbed 'Star Wars' by the press – which was aimed at developing a space-based missile-defence capability.[47] In 1987, Nakasone also secured cabinet approval to raise defence spending – albeit by a tiny amount – above the self-imposed cap of 1% of GNP. Nakasone was also voluble in his support for constitutional revision, which included amending Article 9 and clarifying the constitutional status of the SDF, although pragmatically he recognised the political difficulties of achieving this.[48] For all Nakasone's activism, however, it is difficult to discern a specifically geo-economic element to his policy. Indeed, much of his administration's energy with regards to economic policy was consumed with placating increasing tensions with the US over the size of Japan's trade surplus.[49]

Since the end of the Cold War, three LDP-led administrations have sought to challenge Japan's post-Second World War security trajectory. Externally, in addition to a desire never to repeat the diplomatic trauma of the first Gulf War (in which constitutional and political wrangling saw Japan's response limited to a financial contribution to the coalition), the first North Korean nuclear crisis of 1992–94 and the third Taiwan Strait crisis of 1995–96 were also a major trigger for fresh security-policy initiatives after the LDP's return to power in 1996, particularly for upgrading Japan's security relationship with the US.[50] Domestically, power shifts within the LDP provided further momentum for change. The discrediting and weakening of the LDP's long-dominant dovish wing, which had presided over the party's 1993 fall from power as well as the bursting of the asset-price bubble, and the parallel rise of its hawkish, revisionist wing, which sought to free Japan from its post-Second World War constitutional constraints, provided an important political tailwind for this.[51]

The first of these administrations was that of Hashimoto Ryutaro in 1996–98. The major foreign-policy achievement of the Hashimoto premiership was to preside over the first revision to the Guidelines for Japan–US Defense Cooperation since they were first issued in 1978.[52] The new guidelines envisaged greater burden-sharing by Tokyo through allowing it to respond militarily to contingencies arising from 'situations around Japan'. This was an important evolution from the 1978 guidelines, which had focused largely on the defence of Japan itself. But Hashimoto's window of opportunity was short. Economic instability following the 1997 Asian financial crisis, which damaged Japan's interests in the region, and increasing problems in Japan's own financial sector following the bursting of Japan's economic bubble in the early 1990s contributed to the brevity of his premiership. Hashimoto resigned in July 1998, taking responsibility for a disastrous showing by the LDP in the mid-year Diet (parliament) upper-house election.

Another external shock, the 11 September 2001 terror attacks on the US, triggered a further step change in Japan's security policy under the 2001–06 administration led by Koizumi Junichiro. In 2004, Christopher Hughes accurately referred to the Koizumi administration's response to the US-led 'war on terror' as 'unprecedented'.[53] A desire in Tokyo to avoid repeating the reputational trauma of the first Gulf War was a strong catalyst for the focus and speed of Koizumi's response. In October 2001 the Diet passed the Anti-Terrorism Special Measures Law, and in November 2001 Japan sent the Maritime Self-Defense Force (MSDF, Japan's de facto navy) to the Indian Ocean to provide logistical support for the US-led coalition's operations in Afghanistan.[54] In 2004, the Ground Self-Defense Force (GSDF) and the Air Self-Defense Force (ASDF) were deployed in Iraq and Kuwait under the 'Special Measures on Humanitarian and Reconstruction Assistance in Iraq' Law passed by the Diet in December 2003.[55] This was the first international deployment by the SDF that was not under a UN mandate. Other changes under the Koizumi administration included a decision in December 2003 to build a ballistic-missile-defence (BMD) system, which in effect committed Japan to technological and strategic alignment on missile defence with the US, and revisions in 2004 to Japan's basic defence policy (the National Defense Program Guidelines) and the five-year implementation plan for this policy (the Mid-Term Defense Program).[56]

Thanks in part to Japanese support given to the US after the 2001 terror attacks, US–Japan economic relations were relatively smooth during the Koizumi years – certainly in comparison with the strains of the 1980s and early 1990s. By contrast, relations with China and South Korea cooled under the Koizumi administration. A particular cause of this was the prime minister's visits to the controversial Yasukuni Shrine, where the spirits of Japan's military war dead are enshrined, including those of 14 officers convicted of being 'Class-A' war criminals after the Second World War.[57] Cooler relations with Beijing and Seoul impeded Japan's ability to project broader influence into much of the region.[58]

Abe's structural break

Building on the Hashimoto and Koizumi reforms, the second administration of Abe Shinzo (2012–20) ushered in some of Japan's most far-reaching security-policy changes since 1945. The pace of these reforms is striking even in an international context and reflected both the lessons learned by Abe from the policy failures of his 2006–07 administration as well as the ideological urgency of wanting to restore the Japanese autonomy ('Nihon ga dokuritsu wo torimodosu') that he believed was lost after the Second World War, thus reforming the 'post-war regime' (sengo rejīmu kara no dakkyaku)[59] and allowing Japan to return to global 'Tier 1' status.[60] Related to this was his identification of China, and its widening sphere of influence in the region and drive for great-power status, as the biggest strategic threat to Japan.[61] In some respects, Abe was just the latest in a long line of Japanese leaders for whom China was a 'political obsession' in one way or another.[62] Given its size, impact on the region and the two countries' shared history and geographical proximity, China has unsurprisingly exerted a strong gravitational pull on Japanese politics and even national identity.[63] But Abe's desire to confront a rising China from a position of reinvigorated national strength as a way of preserving regional stability – which reflected his view that underestimating the strength and resolution of one power by another is a major cause of conflict – was new.[64] The approach made strategic sense for Japan given both its geographical proximity to China and what Australian international-relations scholar Coral Bell, writing in the late 1960s, aptly and presciently termed China's 'tenacity':

> China has been a very tenacious power: tenacious of its people ...; tenacious, at least in intention, of territory acquired (an area won for civilization – that is for China – was not to be considered permanently lost, even if temporarily out of control); tenacious of old scores ...[65]

Despite his political dominance in his second administration, and his implementation of a flurry of significant security reforms, Abe still failed to achieve his signature ambition of changing Article 9 of the constitution.[66] This reflected both the very high procedural hurdles to revision and the lack of a clear public majority in favour of it.

Abe's overall vision also contained economic underpinnings for reinforcing national strength. Domestically, this found expression in his 'Abenomics' internal balancing policy platform, announced in 2013. While enjoying some success, Abe's domestic economic policies have had a mixed legacy. Abe had more success with his economic foreign policy and diplomacy. His bid to restore 'Japanese autonomy' saw a step change from previous administrations in the deployment of

Japanese economic statecraft overseas. One change involved a concerted effort to build coalitions of like-minded partners with a view to supporting the rules-based international order. The importance of rules in Abe's policy strategy was underscored in the title of his keynote address to the 13th IISS Shangri-La Dialogue in June 2014: 'Japan for the rule of law. Asia for the rule of law. And the rule of law for all of us.'[67] Leading examples of this coalition-building included: the Partnership for Quality Infrastructure, in collaboration with the ADB and announced shortly after Chinese President Xi Jinping's 2013 BRI launch (2014); the Free and Open Indo-Pacific (FOIP), which provided, among other things, an organising framework for Japan's economic statecraft in the region (2016); Japan's successful rescue of the Trans-Pacific Partnership (TPP) regional trade mega-deal after US withdrawal and its rebirth as the Comprehensive and Progressive Agreement for Trans-Pacific Partnership (CPTPP) (2017); and the securing of G20 support at the Osaka Summit for Japan's quality infrastructure policy and the launch of the Osaka Track to promote the Data Free Flow with Trust (DFFT) concept to, respectively, counter China's BRI and push for 'internet sovereignty' (2019). The addition of an economics unit to the new inter-agency National Security Secretariat (NSS) to coordinate economic security affairs in 2020 marked an important institutional strengthening of the Japanese government's ability to coordinate responses to economic security challenges, which overlapped with geo-economic concerns such as supply-chain security.

Externally, Abe was able to use Trump's hard line against China as a cover for rallying support for Japan's efforts to build China-balancing coalitions, combining openness to China in order to help preserve the liberal international order (through, for example, FOIP – which Tokyo views as being open to Beijing, at least in theory – and the CPTPP) with an implicit message of deterrence (through, for example, the Quadrilateral

Security Dialogue, known as the Quad, with Australia, India and the US, and Japan's own security reforms).[68]

The activism of Abe's foreign policy was thus partly a response to China's rise and its impact on the balance of power in Asia. In this he was an early mover by the standards of, for example, his G7 peers – his identification of the threat China posed to Japan was already apparent at the time of his first, short-lived 2006–07 administration, notwithstanding China's then generally benign global posture and the still favourable world economic environment. For example, in his de facto 2006 manifesto, *Utsukushii Kuni E* ('Towards a Beautiful Country'), he wrote at some length on China, citing the uneven domestic distribution of China's rapid economic growth and Chinese antagonism towards Japan, while acknowledging the 'inseverable' interdependence of the Sino-Japanese economic relationship in a striking phrase: *'Nihon to Chūgoku wa kitte mo kirenai "gokei no kankei" ni aru no ron wo matanai'* (There is no arguing that Japan–China relations are unseverable and reciprocal).[69] All this did not, however, prevent him from remaining open to improving relations with Beijing – witness his first term wherein he tried to repair the damage done to bilateral relations during the Koizumi administration by visiting China on his first overseas trip in October 2005, or during his second term, when, for example, in November 2014 Japan and China were able to agree on four underpinning principles for future dialogue, or towards the end of his premiership when he sought to secure a state visit by President Xi to Japan in 2020, despite Tokyo's concerns about China's territorial probing around the Senkaku/Diaoyu islands.[70]

Abe's interrelated internal and external balancing and coordination of Japanese foreign policy across the economic and security spheres to position Japan as a protector of the rules-based order, thus supplementing US power in Asia to balance a rising, revisionist China, already marks him out as one of Japan's most consequential post-Second World War prime ministers, despite the patchy record of 'Abenomics'.[71] Although his immediate successor, Suga Yoshihide, did not enjoy anything like the same degree of political dominance as Abe, there was little deviation under Suga from the broad course set by his predecessor, notwithstanding his politically pragmatic downgrading of the urgency of constitutional reform. Initial signals from the succeeding administration of Kishida Fumio, who became prime minister in October 2021, also suggested broad foreign-policy continuity. Although the pace of innovation may slow in the absence of a leader as electorally dominant and secure as Abe was during his second administration, geo-economics as a key ingredient in Japanese statecraft looks as if it is here to stay.

Considering Japan's geo-economic effectiveness

This *Adelphi* book will, however, attempt to answer a larger and, for Japan's partners, more consequential question than that of the durability of Japan's geo-economic activity – that of how effective Tokyo can be as a geo-economic actor given the constraints on Japan's full-spectrum power projection; or, phrased differently: although Abe recognised Japan's responsibility to support the rules-based order, to what extent did he enhance Japan's ability to act in support of this goal? To answer this question, it is important to consider the triggers for Japan's refining of its geo-economic strategy. We will look at the means by which Japan has sought to pursue geo-economic power and how its conceptualisation of economic statecraft has changed since 1945, and we will offer an assessment of how successful this pursuit has been.

This assessment will also examine a number of Japanese-specific obstacles, in terms of institutions, domestic ideological tensions, capabilities and resilience, to Tokyo's employment of geo-economic power. Japan's ability to facilitate military–civil interaction, given the tight ring-fencing of its defence sector from the civilian economy, will be an important focus of our consideration of Japan's geo-economic power-projection capabilities. Civilian emerging technologies increasingly have military applications, while also being critical for economic growth. Coupled with the military–civil fusion strategy pursued under Xi Jinping in his drive to secure great-power status for China, this has forced the issue to the centre of Japanese geo-economic policymaking.[72] Japan's ongoing difficulty in employing all the militarily-related policies available to a 'normal' state, including greater military–civil interaction, hampers its pursuit of economic security which is, in turn, a key ingredient in geo-economic effectiveness.

Ultimately, the question is whether Japan can become a more effective geo-economic power despite the headwinds. We assume that the changes implemented under Abe's second administration are robust enough to withstand a degree of domestic political fluctuation. Japan is unlikely to revert to being a 'quietist' state in which Tokyo pursues only minimum power-projection capabilities and remains static and reactive to a changing geopolitical and geo-economic environment.[73] Indeed, to do so would suggest acquiescence by Tokyo in Chinese regional hegemony, which looks unlikely given the challenge this would pose politically and economically to the traditional supporters of Japanese prosperity and the rise (according to public-opinion surveys) in voters' concerns about China's behaviour in the region.[74]

We also view as unlikely a revolutionary scenario in which Japan increases its ability to project autonomous power by, for example, acquiring offensive capabilities. This scenario would have the greatest potential for accelerating developments in the technology sector, and hence Japanese geo-economic effectiveness. It would, however, require Japan to dismantle its 'peace constitution' and possess 'normal' military power-projection capabilities as well as to revitalise its defence industry. This could not be done without significant domestic political backlash.

More likely is a scenario in which Japan projects geo-economic power in coordination with the US and Tokyo's close partners through the enhancement of economic inter-operability and plays an active role in setting rules, standards and norms for regional and global trade agreements and new domains such as digital, cyber and space. Under this scenario Japan would, in effect, be duplicating its military-alliance management activities with the US in the economic realm. We argue that Japan can be both evolutionary and effective as a geo-economic actor, albeit less effective than it would be under the less plausible revolutionary outcome.

Finally, we intend this *Adelphi* book to contribute to the literature on Japan's 'grand strategy' in several ways. Firstly, it draws on diverse disciplinary areas, including economics, political economy, foreign policy and security policy, thereby filling what is in our view a gap in the existing literature. Secondly, this book will be one of the first to examine Japan's geo-economic power in the context of great-power compe-tition between the US and China. Underpinning this is a recognition that Japan requires a different strategy from that of the Cold War, because China as a revisionist power is fully embedded in the global economy. Thirdly, Japan boasts a rich seam of analytical literature going back decades which consid-ers global 'power economics' and Japan's place in the world. This includes a number of distinguished Japanese scholars who have written over the years for the IISS *Adelphi* series. This, together with interviews with senior Japanese policy-makers and experts, has informed our research. We hope that this book will also serve to highlight some of Japan's own thinking on this important subject and inform policymakers elsewhere as they grapple with similar issues. In addition, we believe that Japan's path towards geo-economic effectiveness, in an international environment increasingly dominated by the US and the emerging economic superpowers of China and India, can provide useful insights for other 'middle powers' in the coming decades.

CHAPTER ONE

Japan's geo-economic evolution

Japan's journey as an independent geo-economic actor began in the mid-1950s following its post-war reconstruction and return to the international economic system. Japan's military capabilities were fully dismantled after 1945 as part of the Allied powers' broad 'demilitarization and democratization' reforms which were designed to prevent Japan's 'will to war' from re-emerging to challenge the US-led post-war order.[1] Japan's new constitution embodied this in its Article 9 renunciation of war. The demilitarisation programme was, however, halted with the start of the Cold War. The establishment of a Communist regime in China in 1949, quickly followed by the Korean War from 1950–53, dramatically changed Asia's strategic environment. This triggered a course reversal by the US in favour of rebuilding Japan's economic and military capabilities to turn it into an anti-communist bulwark for the region. Even so, this did not mean that the US envisioned a robust and independent military role for Japan – witness the US–Japan mutual defence treaty of 1951, which was partly seen by Washington as a tool for controlling and managing its relations with Tokyo.[2]

Figure 2: **Japanese and Chinese defence spending compared**

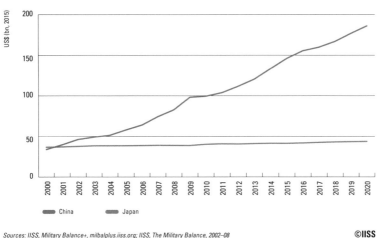

Sources: IISS, Military Balance+, milbalplus.iiss.org; IISS, The Military Balance, 2002–08   ©IISS

This subordinate relationship in security justified the 'mercantilist view of international politics' (*shōninteki kokusai seiji kan*), prioritising Japan's economic growth over full remilitarisation, held by Yoshida Shigeru, prime minister from 1946–47 and 1948–54.[3] The Korean War, during which Japan served as a manufacturing base for US defence equipment, turbocharged Japan's post-war economic recovery. Japan's production surpassed the pre-war level in October 1950, and in fiscal year 1951/52 export volumes rose by a factor of five and import volumes by a factor of three.[4] The Economic Planning Agency's 1956 white paper, which stated that Japan's economy 'is no longer considered to be in a post-war reconstruction period', may be seen as the start of Japan's ability to look outward for economic expansion and to integrate itself into post-war US-led international economic agreements and institutions.[5] The formal ending of the Allied occupation in 1952 (when the San Francisco Peace Treaty came into effect) and Japan's entry into the institutions of the Bretton Woods international monetary system – Japan joined the IMF and the World Bank in 1952 and

Figure 3: **Annual growth in real GDP and consumer price inflation, Japan, 1961–2020**

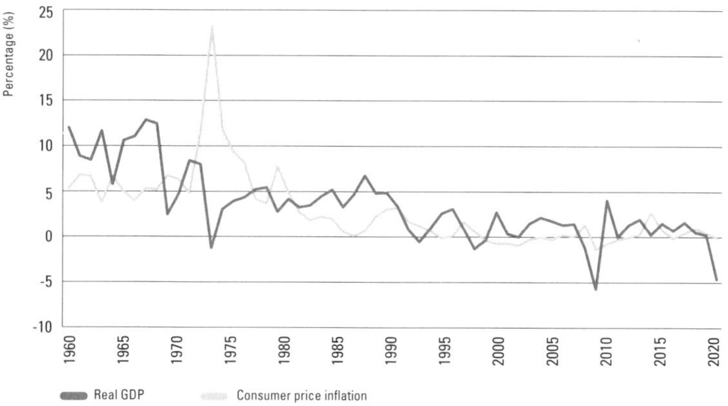

Real GDP   Consumer price inflation

Source: World Bank database   ©IISS

the General Agreement on Tariffs and Trade (GATT) in 1955 – were also important political and economic markers for Japan's return to the international community.

The high-growth era, which lasted from the mid-1950s until the first oil shock of 1973, saw Japan's real GDP grow by an average of 10% per year, an astonishing rate of expansion for an already advanced industrial economy. By 1968, Japan's GDP had become the world's second largest, overtaking that of West Germany.[6] This growing global economic power was a trigger for Japan to begin developing a geo-economic role in Asia, and the Ministry of Foreign Affairs (MOFA) formulated policies intended to support regional states' economic development. Japan's regional role, buoyed by Tokyo's ODA from the 1950s – initially in the form of wartime reparation payments – grew in tandem with Japan's economic weight.[7] Japan's accession in 1960 to both the Organisation for European Economic Cooperation's newly established Development Assistance Group (DAG, now the OECD's Development Assistance Committee) and to the International Development Association, an affiliate of the World

Bank, bolstered its international presence.[8] Japan's initiative in establishing the ADB in 1966 was another example of Tokyo's active regional geo-economic role.

Notwithstanding rising activity, Tokyo's record of achievements in the period was mixed. The Ministerial Conference for the Economic Development of Southeast Asia (SEAMCED), which Tokyo intended as a tool of regional integration, is a good example of this. Tokyo convened SEAMCED in 1966, its first such international initiative since the end of the Second World War, but, notwithstanding the geopolitical headwinds in the region at the time – this was at the height of the Vietnam War – the Conference's failure to gain diplomatic traction suggested that Japan had neither the capacity nor the will to take a leading role in building regional order.[9] Still-fresh memories of the rapacious behaviour of the Imperial Japanese army in Southeast Asia during the Second World War and of Japan's wartime efforts at regional economic integration through its Greater East Asia Co-Prosperity Sphere contributed to regional reluctance to engage with the initiative. At SEAMCED's second meeting in the Philippine capital Manila, for example, the Philippines' president Ferdinand Marcos warned against attempts by any country to dominate the region economically.[10] SEAMCED only met until 1974.

Domestic ideological friction and US ambivalence about Japan building a regional role for itself also constrained Tokyo's room for manoeuvre in the period. After the US entry into the Vietnam War in 1965, for example, Washington wanted Tokyo to play a more active economic role in the region as its ally. But political divisions within Japan regarding its security alliance with the US circumscribed Tokyo's ability to give support to this idea. At times, the US also limited Japan's exercise of geo-economic power. Under prime minister Ikeda Hayato (in office 1962–64), Tokyo began engaging with China. This reflected his view that establishing formal ties with Beijing, not Taipei, would become the future trend.[11] He began the engagement economically by signing a memorandum for 'friendly trade' between private firms in 1962, despite the intense hostility between the US and China.[12] Japan's political room for manoeuvre with regard to China was, however, constrained by its need to align diplomatically with the US in the anti-communist war in Vietnam and by its desire to avoid controversy with its ally, particularly in order to secure Washington's agreement to return Okinawa to Japanese sovereignty, which it accomplished in 1972.[13]

Tectonic changes in the 1970s

International political and economic turbulence in the 1970s prompted a major shift in Japan's geo-economic strategy, particularly in terms of needing to build economic security and resilience. There were three main triggers for this change. The first two came in the form of the two unilateral moves by US president Richard Nixon in 1971 that triggered structural breaks in US policy, known in Japan as the 'Nixon shocks' (*Nikuson shokku*). The first of these came in July 1971 with Nixon's announcement that his national security advisor, Henry Kissinger, had secretly visited China – with which the US did not yet have diplomatic relations – to prepare the ground for a presidential visit to Beijing with the aim of normalising bilateral ties, with Nixon subsequently visiting Beijing in February 1972. This US volte face on China policy, designed to offset the United States' weakening position in the region as a result of its Vietnam War setbacks and to increase US leverage against the Soviet Union, was a brutal reminder to Japan of its lack of agency in its relationship with the US – prime minister Sato was informed only minutes before Nixon's announcement. Japan was, however, subsequently quick to adjust its policy towards China, restoring diplomatic relations with Beijing in September 1972 (more than eight years ahead of the US) under Sato's successor as prime minister, Tanaka Kakuei (in office 1972–74), thus paving the way for a significant and successful deepening of Sino-Japanese economic relations in the late 1970s and 1980s.

The second shock came in August 1971 with Nixon's suspension of the convertibility of the US dollar to gold and the introduction of a 10% surcharge on imports into the US. Japan and others had prospered under the global fixed exchange-rate regime, which had also underpinned the post-Second World War Bretton Woods international monetary system and had been underwritten by post-war US economic strength. By 1970, however, rising inflation, fiscal and trade deficits and unemployment in the US had drained Washington's ability to support this global economic role.[14] Nixon's striking down of this system against the background of his desire to extricate the US from the Vietnam War fed already heightened Japanese concerns about the reliability of its strategic relationship with the US. With his second shock Nixon was 'in essence telling the world that the near omnipotent role that the United States had played since the war was over'.[15]

The third trigger was the Yom Kippur War between a coalition of Arab states on the one hand and Israel on the other in October 1973 and the accompanying embargo on oil exports by the Organization of the Petroleum Exporting Countries (OPEC) to those countries seen as supporting Israel, including Japan. This 'first oil shock' – with the second one coming in 1979 after the Iranian Revolution – and the resulting steep increase in global oil prices hit Japan's oil-intensive economy hard, revealing the extreme vulnerability of its economic health to external geopolitical events. (At the time, Japan's oil-import dependency was 99.7%, of which 88% came from the Middle East.)[16] The rise in oil prices fuelled already building inflationary pressures in Japan, tipping the country into its deepest recession since 1945. But global economic turmoil also catalysed Japan's global economic role. One example of this was the convening in 1975 of the first G6 meeting, which included Japan as well as France, Italy, the UK, the US and West Germany, and was designed to explore solutions to what was then seen as the steepest global economic downturn since the 1930s.[17]

Apart from precipitating its 1973–74 recession, the 'first oil shock' was significant for Japan as it signalled the beginning of an era of global 'power economics', in which economic rather than military power and tools became a major focus of state-craft.[18] In Japan, this manifested itself in two major ways. The first was the development of Japan's first post-1945 regional geo-economic strategy for Southeast Asia. The strategy, called the Fukuda Doctrine after its originator, prime minister Fukuda Takeo (in office 1976–78), and outlined by him on a visit to Manila in 1977, stated three pillars for Japanese policy towards Southeast Asia: the rejection of a military role for Japan in the region; the consolidation of Japan's relationship with the region through 'heart to heart' understanding; and the positioning of Japan as an 'equal partner' of Southeast Asian countries and their regional grouping, the Association of Southeast Asian Nations (ASEAN). This was significant for Japan's geo-economic strategy in two ways.[19] First, it reconfirmed to Southeast Asian governments that Japan intended to play a geo-economic rather than a military role in their region. Second, the Fukuda Doctrine pointed to a repositioning of Japan's engagement in Southeast Asia away from a narrow, bilaterally based commercial focus. One important result of the Doctrine was an increased Japanese focus on Southeast Asia when allocating ODA: in 1977 Tokyo announced that it would double its ODA to the region by 1980.[20]

In contrast with the mid-1960s when Japan's evolving ambitions outpaced its limited resources, as for example with SEAMCED, the Fukuda Doctrine suggested a step change in both Japan's capacity and its political will to play a geo-economic role in the region. The efforts by Fukuda's successor as prime minister, Ohira Masayoshi (in office 1978–80), which included setting up a Pacific Basin Cooperation Study Group (*Kan Taiheiyō Rentai Kenkyū Gurupu*) in 1979 to consider policy towards the region, and launching a joint initiative with Australia to establish the Pacific Economic Cooperation Council (PECC) in 1980, were a continuation of the Fukuda Doctrine's geo-economic push.[21]

The second manifestation of 'power economics' was the emergence of a Japanese national security strategy that for the first time integrated 'comprehensive security' (*sōgō anzenhoshō*) into traditional security thinking. Comprehensive security included non-military threats to Japan's economic welfare, such as energy and food security. In the late 1970s, Fukuda, Ohira and Nakasone Yasuhiro (who was prime minister from 1982–87) had all linked securing natural-resource supplies for the Japanese economy with national security.[22] However, it was Ohira who conceptualised the term – witness his manifesto for the leadership election of the ruling LDP in 1978:

> Japan must ensure its security by establishing a comprehensive security system based on a peace strategy. In other words, while maintaining the current collective security system – the combination of the Japan–US Security Treaty and moderate, but quality self-defence capabilities – Japan should complement this system by enhancing its domestic affairs in various areas, such as the economy, education and culture, and by making the necessary diplomatic efforts, such as existing economic

cooperation and cultural diplomacy. This is a comprehensive approach to measure Japan's security.[23]

In 1979, Ohira set up a study group on comprehensive security (*Sōgō Anzenhoshō Kenkyū Gurūpu*), led by two of Japan's top political scientists at the time, Inoki Masamichi and the aforementioned Kosaka Masataka. The study group produced a report in 1980 that combined military and economic elements of security under Ohira's comprehensive security concept, emphasising the need for Japan to take on greater security and economic roles as a 'member of the West' in a strategic environment that had shifted from 'peace by the US (Pax Americana)' to one of 'peace through shared responsibility'.[24] The ideas presented in the report were not officially used by Ohira, as he died suddenly in 1980; however, they did reflect Tokyo's evolving strategic thinking on how Japan could employ geo-economic instruments to play an active role in maintaining the post-Second World War order.[25]

The 1980s and early 1990s: the limits of 'low posture'
As late as 1980, despite Japan's transformed global economic importance and an emergent evolution in its geo-economic thought, Miyazawa Kiichi, a leading proponent of the Yoshida Doctrine's 'low posture' – who was then a senior figure in Japan's long-ruling LDP and later the prime minister who presided over the party's fall from power in July 1993 – was still able to say that Tokyo's foreign policy

precludes all value judgements. It is a pretence of foreign policy. The only value judgements we can make are determining what is in Japan's best interest. Since there are no real value judgements possible, we cannot say anything … All we can do when we are hit on the head is pull back. We follow the world situation and follow the trends.[26]

This self-perception, and the broad continuity in Japanese post-war foreign policy, encouraged charges that Japan was reactive and, particularly regarding its policy towards the US, mercantilist: Japan benefited from the US-led international order, but did not contribute to its maintenance.[27] The aftermath of the 1985 Plaza Accord between the central-bank governors and finance ministers of the G5 – France, Germany, Japan, the UK and the US – provided an example of Japan's reactiveness. Although Japan was not alone in acquiescing to pressure from Washington for an exchange-rate adjustment to help the US reduce its large current-account deficits, the 1980s had seen a sharp increase in US–Japan trade friction, particularly in strategically important sectors such as cars and semiconductors. In the event, the yen bore the brunt of the appreciation, strengthening from ¥237:US$1 at end-August just ahead of the meeting to ¥168:US$1 by end-April 1986 and to ¥126:US$1 by end-1988.[28] In the year to April 1986, the yen had appreciated by an astonishing nearly 30% in nominal-effective terms, compared with a 10% appreciation for Germany's deutsche mark, which was the other G5 currency significantly affected.[29]

The appreciation gave Japan an enormous increase in spending power almost overnight. One observer describes how Japan 'inadvertently acquired extreme purchasing power just by sleeping'.[30] It did not, however, have a significant impact on the trade imbalance in Tokyo's favour between the US and Japan. In engineering the yen's appreciation, Japan not only in effect ceded control over the important monetary-policy lever of domestic economic policy, but also lit the touchpaper that led to the asset-price bubble of the late 1980s.[31] It also fuelled an investment binge on overseas trophy assets, particularly in the real-estate sector, many of which were disposed of in the 1990s as domestic economic distress took hold.[32] It is worth noting that China, which like Japan previously has also experienced rapid economic growth, appears to have learned from Japan's currency lurches and has been tightly managing the renminbi's rise against the US dollar since its first major currency-policy reform for a decade in 2005.[33]

Although Japan began to link its economic and security interests with its policies from the late 1970s, Tokyo's strategy initially fell short of addressing this convergence in a particularly important area: the protection and development of dual-use technologies.[34] This was partly a legacy of Japan's post-1945 separation of the security and economic spheres, which had undermined its institutional ability to understand the security implications of technologies that were created by civilian high-technology firms. But three events, two in the 1980s and one in the early 1990s, increased awareness in Tokyo that failure to recognise this convergence could threaten or limit Japan's geo-economic power-projection capacity.

The first event was a Japanese defence contractor's export of sensitive technology to the Soviet Union. In 1987, a whistle-blower revealed that between 1981 and 1984 Toshiba Machine, a subsidiary of leading Japanese technology firm Toshiba, had, together with the state-owned Norwegian defence firm Kongsberg Våpenfabrikk, been exporting a computer-guided propeller milling machine to the Soviet Union that could significantly enhance the operational effectiveness of Soviet submarine systems.[35] This was a violation of the export controls of the multinational Coordinating Committee for Multilateral Export Control (CoCom), the purpose of which was to prevent the Soviet Union from acquiring advanced technology and of which Japan was a member. The case triggered punitive action against Toshiba by the Japanese and US governments and, unsurprisingly given strained US–Soviet relations at the time, also damaged Tokyo's relations with Washington as it fuelled the already intensifying 'Japan-bashing' movement and the negative perceptions of Japan in the US originating from the growing trade imbalance between the two countries.[36]

The second event was Japanese defence and electronics company Fujitsu's plan to acquire the US semiconductor firm Fairchild Semiconductor in 1986–87. This came against the backdrop of growing US–Japan trade frictions, which in 1986 led Japan to make concessions to Washington by agreeing to curb its semiconductor exports to the US and third countries voluntarily and to help secure a 20% share of its own market for foreign manufacturers.[37] From Fujitsu's perspective, acquisition of Fairchild Semiconductor would allow it to support its semiconductor business in the US and hence to offset the impact of the 1986 deal. But while the decision had a business rationale for the Japanese firm, for the US this was a takeover of a valuable strategic asset – the 'mother of semiconductors' – at the leading edge of technology.[38] There was significant opposition in the US to Fujitsu's plan, and US president Ronald Reagan ordered tariffs against Japanese products containing semiconductors in retaliation for alleged violation of the 1986 semiconductor deal.[39] It was no coincidence that the two incidents occurred against the backdrop of Japan's ascendance as a dual-use-technology provider and the growing dependence of the US on Japanese technology for its military equipment.

The third event came in the form of the foreign-policy trauma for Tokyo as a result of the first Gulf War of 1990–91. Notwithstanding Japan's overwhelming reliance on oil imports from the Middle East, constitutional and domestic political constraints meant that Tokyo was unable to dispatch the SDF to the Gulf.[40] The extent of its support for the US-led effort was to provide the allies with some material aid and a cash contribution, albeit a substantial one of US$13bn that was larger than Japan's entire annual ODA allocation and required a supplementary budget and a temporary tax increase. Even considerably poorer and economically smaller South Korea and the Philippines were able to provide a greater 'human contribution' in the form of military medical units.[41] Japan's failure to share the burden of the conflict more comprehensively meant that Tokyo received scant international gratitude for its financial contribution to the war effort. Rather, international commentary focused on Japan's 'chequebook diplomacy' and the narrowness of its interests.[42] This episode shone a harsh light on the disconnect between Japan's economic clout and its ability to play a full-spectrum international role. Tokyo's passivity and reactiveness was all the more striking given the open violation of international law – the upholding of which had supported Japanese prosperity – presented by Iraq's invasion of Kuwait and the United Nations' authorisation of 'all necessary means' by member states to secure the withdrawal of Iraqi forces from Kuwait.[43]

Japan's policy swing in the 1990s and an evolving view of China
US–Japan friction immediately after the end of the Cold War was driven in part by US perceptions of Japan as an unfair economic competitor, and the associated 'threat to American economic primacy from Japan', as well as US disappointment over Japan's Gulf War contribution.[44] Although the bursting of Japan's asset bubble in 1990 and the economic malaise that set in during the second half of the 1990s weakened Japan's geo-economic power-projection capabilities, Tokyo remained active in Asia. The Asia-Pacific Economic Cooperation (APEC) forum, set up in 1989 on the initiative of Australia and Japan, was a potential means of keeping the US engaged politically and economically in the region and, after China's accession

in 1991, of providing a forum for engaging Beijing as well as Washington on regional issues. Indeed, APEC was an early recognition of China's rising importance in the region. The Asian financial and economic crises of 1997–98 spurred Tokyo's development of a regional approach to stabilise Asia's tottering economies, which included the ultimately abortive initiative to set up an Asian Monetary Fund (AMF) and the AMF's more successful follow-up, the Chiang Mai Initiative (CMI).[45]

From the 1990s, the evolution of Tokyo's view of China – from partner to competitor – became a central theme in Japanese geo-economic thinking. China's economy had developed rapidly in the wake of reforms initiated by Deng Xiaoping in 1978. Optimists in the West believed that China would rise peacefully within the US-led liberal economic system.[46] Chinese accession to the WTO in 2001 and the ensuing brisk growth of trade and deepening economic interdependence between Japan and China appeared to confirm the view in Tokyo that China would be an important partner for Japan in shaping the region's economic order. The supporters of this view observed that China was still a relatively small geo-economic power, and that it would take decades for it to become large enough to pose a threat to Japan or to the United States' political and economic positions in Asia.[47]

Some in the security-policy community in Japan were, however, more cautious about the trajectory of China's rise. Japan's policy hawks cited the fundamental differences between the two countries' ideological, political and economic systems, and warned that China's economic growth could cause strategic and security challenges for Japan.[48] The massacre of anti-government demonstrators by Chinese state security forces in Beijing in June 1989 was more evidence for the hawks of the incompatibility of China's political system with democratic values. Chinese President Jiang Zemin's initiation of patriotic education in Chinese schools from 1994, China's nuclear tests in 1995, the second Taiwan Strait crisis in 1995–96 and China's increasing readiness to press Japan on differences over shared history, all pointed to Beijing's rising confidence in its ability to influence the regional order.[49] China's rapid growth after its accession to the WTO also eroded Japan's economic primacy in the region at astonishing speed – having been one-quarter the size of Japan's economy on the eve of its WTO accession in 2001, by 2010 China had overtaken Japan – adding grist to the mill of those in Tokyo worried about China's place in the regional order.[50]

The policy swings between different Japanese prime ministers in the first decade of the twenty-first century reflected these differing views on China. Prime ministers from the right-leaning LDP, notably Koizumi Junichiro (in office 2001–06) and his successor, Abe Shinzo, in his first administration (2006–07), took a firmer approach to China in order to protect Japan's ability to shape the regional geo-economic order. When Sino-Japanese bilateral relations deteriorated in the early 2000s owing to both sides' hardening nationalism and their digging in on their respective positions on wartime history, Koizumi made no concessions to China. As prime minister he continued his controversial visits to the Yasukuni Shrine even at the cost of a sharp deterioration in relations with Beijing.

While recognising the political and security challenges resulting from China's rise, Abe moved to defuse tensions, acknowledging the importance of ties with Beijing. Abe even went as far as agreeing in the Japan–China Joint Press Statement after his visit to Beijing in 2006 to turn the East China Sea into a 'Sea of Peace, Cooperation and Friendship' – a formulation that has not aged well given Japan's rising concerns over the following decade concerning China's increasingly aggressive promotion of its territorial claims in the sea.[51] Thus the framework for bilateral relations that Japan adopted in 2006 – a 'mutually beneficial rela-

Figure 4: **Japan–India top-level bilateral visits, 1980–2020**

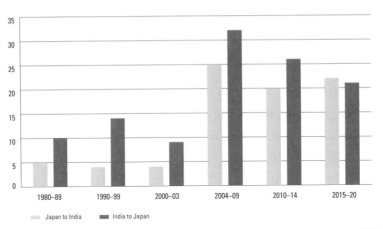

Source: Japan, Ministry of Foreign Affairs   ©IISS

tionship based on common strategic interest' (*senryaku teki gokei kankei*)[52] – reflected Japan's desire to build a constructive relationship with China, although, in Abe's thinking, this needed to be done from a position of strength through the improvement of Japan's own defence capabilities and of the US–Japan Alliance.

During Abe's first administration, growing wariness about China gave rise to a new Japanese geo-economic strategy for Asia that saw a central role for India in the regional order. Abe's 'Confluence of the Two Seas' speech to the Indian parliament in Delhi in 2007, in which he called for Indo-Japanese cooperation 'for the future of this new "broader Asia"' to 'enrich the seas of freedom and prosperity', reflected this shift.[53] For Abe, India had 'geo-economic synergies' with Japan: it is the world's largest democracy and is on track to be the world's third-largest economy by the middle of the twenty-first century, which stands in stark contrast to Japan's slow-growth economy and ageing population.[54] India was also an important strategic partner for Japan: they shared an important interest in protecting the region's sea lanes. Japan's business ties with India and its support for India's economic development via ODA had already grown since the start of the century. In 2000, the two governments agreed a Japan–India Global Partnership and, since 2003, India has been the top recipient of Japanese ODA.[55] Bilateral ties deepened further after Abe's first premiership, with foreign direct investment from Japan and inter governmental exchanges both rising quickly.

At the other end of Japan's political spectrum, there was a strong appetite for engagement with China to build the regional geo-economic order. Hatoyama Yukio, who was the first of the three left-leaning Democratic Party of Japan (DPJ) prime ministers following the party's electoral victory in 2009 and who held office from 2009–10, promoted the political and economic integration of East Asia – which in his definition included ASEAN, China, Hong Kong, Japan, South Korea and Taiwan – as a pathway for Japan to achieve 'political and economic independence' from both the US and a rising China.[56] Hatoyama was a political idealist who believed that developing an 'East Asian community' and a collective security framework with these countries could help to solve the territorial disputes within the region as the European Union had done for Europe. From a geo-economic perspective, some in Tokyo saw the proposal as an attempt by Hatoyama to integrate an economically expanding China into a Japan-led regional economic architecture in order to prevent the US, which he viewed as a 'unilateral' actor and a declining power particularly since the 2008 global financial crisis, from determining the regional order under a Sino-US condominium.[57] Unsurprisingly, US–Japan relations chilled under Hatoyama, especially after he overturned a bilateral decision made in 2006, and favoured by Washington, to move a US Marine Corps Air Station base from one location to another off the island of Okinawa.[58]

China's twenty-first-century rise: four triggers for Japan's shifting geo-economic perceptions

Although Hatoyama's idea of an 'East Asian Community' echoed earlier initiatives such as APEC and ASEAN + 3, he had misread how China's own view of its regional role had evolved, and also overestimated China's willingness to share regional order-building with Japan. Indeed, China's quick stimulus-driven recovery from the 2008 global financial crisis and its overtaking of Japan in 2010 to become the world's second-largest economy emboldened Beijing to assert its claims to regional leadership much more strongly. This was particularly the case regarding its maritime territorial ambitions and attempts to alter the US-led post-1945 liberal political and economic order. Against this background, during the 2010s four major triggers initiated structural shifts in Japan's geo-economic strategy.

The first trigger was Beijing's reaction after the collision between a Chinese trawler and a Japanese coast-guard patrol boat near the disputed Senkaku/Diaoyu islands on 7 September 2010. After Tokyo detained the captain of the Chinese vessel, Beijing halted rare-earth exports to Japan.[59] The move appeared to target critical sectors of the Japanese economy as the materials were essential to the production of motors, magnets, microchips and semiconductors. This took place alongside large protests at Japanese consulates and manufacturing plants across China as well as the cancellation by Beijing of cultural exchanges. Beijing's response to the incident served as a wake-up call for Tokyo that China was willing to weaponise its economic power and trade relations to promote its territorial ambitions.[60] Beijing's 2012 ban on banana imports from the Philippines amid a stand-off in the South China Sea between Chinese and Philippine naval forces further fuelled concerns in Tokyo about China's intent and capability to use economic coercion tactics in the region, which threatened to undermine the rules-based economic and political order and disrupt the sea lines of communication vital for Japan's economic security.[61]

The second trigger came in 2013 with Beijing's launch of its global investment and development BRI (initially branded 'One Belt, One Road') and its proposal to set up the multi-lateral Asian Infrastructure Investment Bank (AIIB, formally launched in 2016), headquartered in Beijing and intended to provide funding for infrastructure projects in the broad Asian region stretching from the Caucasus and the Middle East to the Southwest Pacific. To their critics, the BRI and the AIIB looked like direct challenges to the existing US- and Japan-led multi-lateral financial institutions in the region such as the ADB, and thus an attempt to challenge the post-1945 political and institutional order in Asia. Japan's failure in 2015 to outbid China to build the first phase of Indonesia's US$6bn Jakarta–Bandung high-speed rail link magnified these worries in Tokyo, particularly given Japan's traditionally close economic links with Indonesia. Beijing's success was seen as a warning of the challenge from China's economic competitiveness.[62]

The strategic implications of China's global infrastructure development also concerned Tokyo. BRI critics saw Chinese infrastructure financing as 'dept-trap diplomacy', through which Beijing was trying to secure political and strategic advantage in economically weak countries: they cited the high cost of Chinese loans and the questionable commercial viability of some of the Chinese-financed projects. One relevant high-profile case involved China's funding of the Hambantota port development in Sri Lanka, Colombo's subsequent difficulties with repayment of the loans to fund the project and Sri Lanka's agreement with Beijing in 2017 under which Beijing would write off the debt in return for 80% control of the port on a 99-year lease.[63] Like its Quad partners Australia, India and the US, Japan kept its distance from the BRI, although it indicated willingness to cooperate on BRI projects where standards meet 'common concepts shared by the international community'.[64] Japan has also not joined the AIIB due to concerns over lending standards and the organisation's potential to undermine US and Japan-led regional institutions such as the ADB.[65] Along with Taiwan, it remains the only Asian country not to have done so.

The third trigger was Japan's uncertainty over the trajectory of the US 'rebalance to the Asia-Pacific' (sometimes referred to as 'the pivot') under president Barack Obama. Since the start of Obama's presidency in 2009, concerns had been growing in Tokyo that his foreign-policy priority of tackling global issues such as the need for recovery from the 2008 global financial crisis, nuclear non-proliferation and climate change would make China, not Japan, the most important strategic partner of the US. Tokyo feared that, under what some observers called a 'G2' framework, the US would make major concessions to China's geopolitical 'core interests' – the East China Sea (including the Senkaku/Diaoyu islands), Taiwan and the South China Sea – to secure China's cooperation on global challenges. The 'pivot', which the State Department announced in 2011, initially allayed some of Tokyo's concerns over Obama's approach.[66] But Chinese President Xi Jinping's exhortation to Obama in June 2013 at the informal Sunnylands summit to 'build a new model of major country relationship' between the US and China, including mutual respect for each other's 'core interests', reignited Tokyo's fears of a G2 condominium.[67]

These fears appeared to be substantiated in November 2013 when Beijing designated an Air Defence Identification Zone (ADIZ) in the East China Sea, threatening 'defensive emergency measures' against foreign aircraft that failed to comply with China's requirements.[68] China's ADIZ included airspace over the disputed Senkaku/Diaoyu islands and over-lapped with one that Japan had established in 1969. Beijing's unilateral move signalled a further intensification of China's 'law-fare' operations around the disputed islands. It also followed shortly after the US national security advisor, Susan Rice, had indicated that the US and China should 'seek to operationalize a new model of major power relations', echoing Xi's Sunnylands initiative and further feeding Japanese strategic concerns over a potential 'G2' based on a Sino-American confluence of interests.[69] These two developments were major triggers for Abe in his second administration to strengthen Japan's own security posture through a series of reforms and to improve relations with the US, which had frayed under the preceding DPJ government.[70] These developments also shaped the Abe administration's view that a strong security underpinning, achieved through both improved national military capabilities and enhanced defence cooperation with the US, would be critical in boosting Japan's ability to engage with China on bilateral and regional political and economic issues from a position of strength.

The fourth trigger was China's rapidly developing technological capability in the digital domain and the multi-dimensional threats to the interests of Japan, the US and their partners that this posed in the economic, political and military spheres. The rapid growth of Chinese telecommunications and information-technology (IT) service platforms around the world and Beijing's protectionist nurturing of indigenous firms under Xi's 'Made in China 2025' industrial strategy, launched in 2015, aggravated economic security concerns for Tokyo in several ways. One was the domination of the fifth-generation (5G) wireless telecommunications market by Chinese firms. The strategic importance of 5G is immense, as the technology will serve as the backbone of the digital economy, connecting not only mobile phones, but also data flows through, for example, the Internet of Things, smart manufacturing, remote medicine and automated vehicles. According to business intelligence firm IHS Markit, two Chinese telecommunications companies, Huawei and ZTE, accounted for just under 50% of the 5G base station global market in 2018, with Eriksson of Sweden and Nokia of Finland accounting for the lion's share of the rest.[71] Japanese firms, meanwhile, held under 1% of the market, according to the same source.

Also important were two changes in Chinese legislation during 2017 that focused Japanese economic and security attention on the rapid expansion of Chinese IT platform providers such as Baidu, Alibaba and Tencent (known collectively as the 'BATs') in Japan and other parts of Asia. The first was the Cyber Security Law, which restricted data flows out of China.[72] The second was the National Intelligence Law, which made it mandatory for Chinese firms and their employees to cooperate with China's security agencies whenever required.[73] China's protectionist approach towards data and the lack of transparency regarding the Chinese state's access to private-sector data directly conflicted with Tokyo's push for open cross-border data transfers and data security within the CPTPP trade bloc. The absence of global Japanese IT platform services comparable in size to China's BATs or their US equivalents, Google, Apple, Facebook and Amazon (collectively known as the GAFA), and Japan's ageing and shrinking population (which put Japan at a disadvantage in terms of data-flow volumes), all accelerated Tokyo's concerns about the links between data and national security. Against this backdrop, in April 2017 Amari Akira – LDP grandee, cabinet veteran and Japanese negotiator of the CPTPP (then the TPP) – set up a Diet group for international rules-making, the *Rūru Keisei Senryaku Giin Renmei*, essentially aimed at preventing

China from shaping the rules of the future economy.[74] Abe's DFFT initiative in 2019 was driven by similar concerns.

Beijing's launch in 2015 of the Digital Silk Road (DSR) strand of the BRI to 'construct a community of common destiny in cyberspace' further raised Japanese fears that China could be spreading its digital infrastructure and technologies as a means of amplifying its geo-economic and geopolitical interests.[75] The most important aspect of this was the DSR's potential, through its global networks, to shape standards for future technologies. Xi's 'China Standard 2035' initiative, which was first floated in 2020, positions China as a shaper of global standards in technology areas such as 5G, AI and cloud computing.[76] The initiative informed Beijing's efforts to strengthen its presence in leadership positions in relevant international institutions: the appointment in 2014 of Zhao Houlin as secretary-general of the UN's information and communication technology agency, the International Telecommunication Union (ITU), the first Chinese national to head the organisation, was a case in point.[77] China's Global Initiative on Data Security, launched in September 2020, and the exclusion of provisions to prohibit data-localisation requirements in the Regional Comprehensive Economic Partnership (RCEP) trade bloc, were both driven by the restriction of China's Cyber Security Law on cross-border data flows.[78] Also of concern for Japan (and many Western countries) was Beijing's 'digital Leninism' – that is, China's ability to proliferate its digitally enabled authoritarian governance model, in which the state controls personal data through technologies such as AI-driven mass surveillance, 'social credit' systems and censorship.[79] Some countries in Southeast Asia and Africa have, for example, begun to install Huawei's surveillance cameras in the name of 'safe city projects'.[80]

On the military-technology front, a growing number of reported cases of Chinese espionage activities against Japanese defence contractors and civilian technology firms and agencies have focused Tokyo's attention on the implications of China's expanding cyber capabilities for Japan's technology competitiveness, especially in dual-use technology. In January 2020, Japanese defence contractor Mitsubishi Electric revealed that a group affiliated with China's People's Liberation Army (PLA) had hacked into its networks, potentially accessing the R&D specifications for a Japanese hypersonic-weapons system along with information on more than 8,000 people connected to the defence ministry.[81] Shortly after this, another Japanese defence contractor, IT giant NEC, disclosed that it had also been hacked.[82] In April 2021, the Japanese Metropolitan Police filed a case against a member of the Chinese Communist Party (CCP) with links to a Chinese hacker group affiliated with the PLA, Tick, for an alleged cyber attack against the Japan Aerospace Exploration Agency (JAXA) in 2016.[83] China has also been seeking to penetrate Japanese academic institutions to gain access to Japan's cutting-edge technologies. In January 2021, the Japanese newspaper *Yomiuri Shimbun* reported that 44 Japanese academics had been involved with China's 'Thousand Talent Plan', in which China gives grants to researchers in advanced technology fields, many of which will have military applications, to go to China to conduct research.[84]

Japan's 'Free and Open Indo-Pacific' concept
China's economic rise and growing political confidence were drivers for the most important geo-economic policy framework of Abe's second administration – the FOIP concept, launched in August 2016 at the Sixth Tokyo International Conference on African Development (TICAD VI) in Kenya. Although, in the US and elsewhere outside Japan, FOIP is often seen as a security construct, it had its origins in geo-economic strategy,[85] as is discussed in greater detail in Chapter Two.[86] FOIP thus

marked a clear expression of intent by Abe that Japan should play the major role that he had articulated in 2013, shortly after returning to office as prime minister, of shaping its external environment as a 'leading promoter of rules' and as a 'guardian of the global commons'.[87]

In this context, the FOIP concept encapsulated three aims for Japan, although these were not directly stated, in relation to shaping Asia's geo-economic environment.[88] The first was to counter what Tokyo saw as China's revisionist challenge to the post-1945 liberal international order that has sustained Japan's economic prosperity and the undermining of which threatens Japan's physical security. Examples of China's unilateral attempts to 'change the status quo' include its irridentism in the East China and South China seas, its use of the BRI to create de facto client states, and its push to influence global standards, particularly in the rapidly evolving digital sector where governance is still weak.[89] FOIP was thus a values-based strategy aimed at maintaining the US-led economic order and upholding international rules in order to prevent overweening behaviour by China. Abe's TICAD VI speech emphasised Japan's wish to make the Indo-Pacific region 'into a place that values freedom, the rule or law, and the market economy, free from force or coercion, and making it prosperous'.[90]

The second aim was to integrate India into this regional geo-economic organising framework. Abe had already catalysed Japan–India relations during his first administration. His return to office in 2012 gave bilateral relations a further boost. As Indian journalist Sanjaya Baru noted, 'it required Abe to return and reiterate Japanese interest'.[91] The launch in November 2012 of negotiations for the RCEP mega trade bloc reinforced India's centrality in Abe's strategy: Japan wanted India to join the bloc as a democratic counterweight to balance China's influence within it – excluding India, China accounts for more than half of RCEP's combined GDP.[92] In the event, however, India has remained outside RCEP, mainly because of New Delhi's concerns about the potential impact of trade liberalisation on its uncompetitive industries in the manufacturing and dairy sectors, particularly with regard to China, which singly accounts for some 40% of India's trade deficit.[93]

The third aim was to embed the US in the regional geoeconomic framework. With its emphasis on democracy, supporting regional connectivity and financial sustainability, FOIP sits in implicit contradistinction to the BRI, which critics see as China-centric and mercantilist. But FOIP is also inclusive by design, remaining open to engagement and cooperation with China. This inclusivity makes strategic sense for Japan, which cannot afford to antagonise China, its largest market. FOIP is also a marked departure from Japan's previous often narrowly focused geo-economic strategy. In contrast, FOIP was supported by the internal and external balancing undertaken in Abe's second administration such as 'Abenomics' to strengthen Japan's economic base; a series of security reforms; and the upgrading of the US–Japan Alliance.[94]

The start of Donald Trump's term as US president in 2017 created internal and external demands for Tokyo to play a still greater geo-economic role under FOIP. Trump's 'America first' approach, which was evident on the first day of his administration when he withdrew the US from the TPP trade bloc ahead of its agreement, was from Tokyo's point of view a threat to the stability of the regional economic order. Including both the US and Japan, who together accounted for 30% of global GDP, the TPP would have had sufficient economic weight to become a powerful economic rule-setter and balancer to China's regional influence.[95] Moreover, the repeated absences of senior Trump administration officials from high-level regional meetings, particularly ASEAN, further undermined the credibility of the US commitment to protect the existing regional order.[96] Concern to preserve the regional economic order's stability persuaded Abe to take the lead in salvaging the deal and in negotiating the TPP's successor, the CPTPP, without the US.

The Trump administration's use of the FOIP formulation, notably in its 2017 National Security Strategy and the 2018 US National Defense Strategy, but also as its signature framework for US policy across this large region, was a major achievement for Tokyo,[97] even though the US version lacked a geo-economic dimension in its early phase.[98] (It was not until secretary of state Mike Pompeo's launch of 'America's Indo-Pacific economic vision' in July 2018 that the US included a geo-economic component, with its setting of three Indo-Pacific priority areas: energy security, infrastructure development and digital connectivity.)[99] However, Trump's fusion of economic and national security in the 2017 security strategy and the ensuing intensification during his administration of US–China strategic competition, which found clearest expression in the sharp ramping up of bilateral trade friction and retaliatory tariffs on key products, created fresh challenges for the liberal international economic order and hence for Japan and its economic resilience, a long-standing component of its geo-economic strategy.[100]

These challenges were in turn aggravated by Trump's persistent unilateralism. US unilateralism is, of course, not new – witness the two Nixon shocks of 1971. But the Trump administration's approach also seemed to contradict the pledge under Article II of the US–Japan Security Treaty that both parties would 'seek to eliminate conflict in their economic policies and ... encourage economic collaboration'.[101] In addition to the example of the US withdrawal from the TPP, another good illustration of US unilateralism was its strengthening of its export and foreign-investment controls, which were often implemented without prior consultations with allies. One such example was the Export Control Reform Act of 2018, which offered a legal basis for the Bureau of Industry and Security within the US Department of Commerce (DOC) to announce new rules designed to tighten exports on non-traditional areas, such as emerging and foundational technologies.[102] The DOC's new announcement in January 2021 that it was adding AI-driven software for geospatial imagery to the new export control came as a surprise for Japanese businesses such as the defence and commercial space-technology firms that used US content for their satellites.[103] In 2020, the US State Department further ramped up its effort to exclude Chinese digital-technology firms from its networks from a diplomatic perspective under its Clean Network initiative and suggested the possibility of expanding its effort to its allies and partners.

The inclusivity of Japan's FOIP, intended to strengthen Japan's economic resilience by allowing it to maintain its economic ties with China, contrasted with the hard line US course towards China. Sino-Japanese rapprochement from October 2018, when Abe visited Beijing to mark the fortieth anniversary of the two countries signing a bilateral Treaty of Peace and Friendship, stood in marked contrast to deteriorating US–China relations at the time. This was a strategic opportunity for Tokyo to play a balancing role between the US and China, whose bilateral friction created space for closer relations between Japan and China. Abe's visit resulted in a series of economic agreements including one on infrastructure cooperation in third countries.[104] Japanese involvement with Chinese projects offered the potential for raising Chinese infrastructure financing and other standards towards the 'quality infrastructure' investment (QII) standards set out by Tokyo (and now supported by the G7 and G20 countries).[105]

Record numbers of Chinese tourists visiting Japan, and their *bakugai* ('explosive') spending in 2019, further underscored the indispensability for Japan of close economic ties with China.[106] In contrast to the US view of China as a strategic competitor, Abe continued to use the 'mutually beneficial relationship on a common strategic interest' formula as the guiding principle for the two countries' relations.[107] Sino-Japanese rapprochement also had a domestic political dimension for Abe: his failure to resolve the territorial dispute with Russia over the Northern Territories/Kuriles had left him in need of a foreign-policy success story to tell the electorate.

Keizai anzenhoshō: Japanese economic security and military–civil integration

Keizai anzenhoshō, a core component of geo-economic strategy for Japan, is often directly translated as 'economic security'. Japanese experts started using the term in the late 1970s, reflecting the need for policies to cope with the political and economic turbulence of the time.[108] The idea also influenced the comprehensive security [*sōgō anzenhoshō*] concept laid out by prime minister Ohira at the end of the 1970s, which was designed to tackle Japan's broad security challenges, including those in non-military fields such as energy. The end of the Cold War in 1990 and the stable growth cycle of 'the Great Moderation' in the US between the mid-1980s and the 2008 global financial crisis together led to a reduced emphasis on economic security issues in Japan and the West during the period.[109] China's rise re-ignited the economic security debate in the 2010s in Japan and elsewhere. However, the new debate has a geo-economic rather than a largely domestic economic-stability focus that aims to address the economic dimension of China's capability to project national power, as well as Beijing's fusion of economic, high-technology and military policy. Japan's still-evolving economic security policy activity has three main prongs.

The first prong has involved updating the post-1945 rules-based economic order to cope with the shifts in the global balance of power occasioned by China's rise and the disruption caused by the so-called fourth industrial revolution (in other words, the growth of the digital economy). Under Abe's second administration, Tokyo placed particular importance on maintaining open cross-border data flows, which it viewed as a key to Japan's own economic prosperity. Indeed, one former senior government official in the Abe administration describes data as the 'oil' of the twenty-first century, with 5G as the 'pipelines' and AI-driven technologies as the new era's 'refineries'.[110] Beijing's push for data sovereignty, its authoritarian model of data governance and its lack of transparency on data access under its National Intelligence Law were thus viewed in Tokyo as economic risks for Japan, and ensuring the free flow of data securely across borders as the most important economic security goal.[111] This explains Tokyo's push for its DFFT concept at the World Economic Forum in 2019 and the launch at the G20 Osaka Summit in the same year of the Osaka Track to promote cross-border data-transfer rules-making under the WTO. With its data focus, Japanese policy diverged somewhat from that of the US, which at the time was still focused on addressing economic security concerns about Chinese dominance of 5G.

The second prong has been the addition of industrial policy goals to achieve economic resilience in sectors and goods that matter for national security. China's halting of rare-earth exports to Japan in 2010 was an important trigger for Japan to develop policy to ensure supply-chain resilience for critical materials and strategic goods. However, Sino-US technology competition and policies adopted by the US and the EU to restrict trade in sensitive technologies – for example, in the areas of telecommunications, semiconductor manufacturing and AI-driven software – forced

Figure 5: **Japan's rare-earth imports from China and other countries, 2010 and 2019**

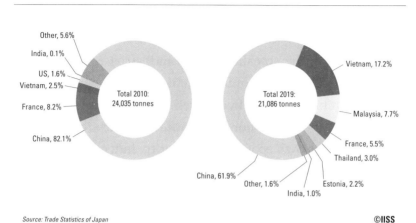

Source: Trade Statistics of Japan   ©IISS

Tokyo to think strategically about boosting domestic manufacturing capabilities for goods that are linked to national security, in addition to efforts to diversify supply chains. The global coronavirus pandemic added medical and health goods to the list of strategic sectors. China, which experienced an early recovery from the COVID-19 pandemic during 2020, deployed its extensive domestic production capabilities and supplies of masks, ventilators and vaccines to exert geo-economic influence in the region and in the world under its so-called 'mask diplomacy' and 'vaccine diplomacy'.[112] Highlighting growing trends towards interventionist policies by China, Europe, the US and other major economies, the policy council of Japan's Ministry of Economy, Trade and Industry (METI), for example, called in June 2021 for Tokyo to embark on 'a new industrial policy from the economic security perspective' (*keizai anzenhoshō no kanten kara no aratana sangyō seisaku*).[113]

The third prong has been to protect and develop critical and emerging technologies that have potential military or other security-related applications. With a shared goal of achieving 'safety and security' through technology, after the 11 September 2001 terrorist attacks on the US the Cabinet

Office, the Ministry of Defense (MOD), METI and the Ministry of Education, Culture, Sports, Science and Technology (MEXT) began to link civilian technologies and national security for the purpose of dealing more effectively with non-traditional security issues such as terrorism, the proliferation of weapons of mass destruction and natural disasters.[114] However, accounts by former government officials, debates in the government's advisory councils as well as relevant government white papers suggest that 2018–19 saw an acceleration in Tokyo's addressing of the challenges arising from Sino-US strategic competition and China's military–civil fusion strategy.[115] For example, Japan's Cabinet put together its first Integrated Innovation Strategy in 2018 to set goals and steps to protect, develop and use emerging technologies.[116] The strategy also stated its aim to contribute to enhancing security in the cyber, maritime and space domains. METI's policy advisory councils and its *White Paper on International Economy* in 2019 echoed this approach and highlighted the need to protect sensitive technologies and industries through a new concept of 'economic policy integrated with security interests' (*anzenhoshō to ittai to natta keizai seisaku*).[117]

Efforts by MOD to deal with China's technological rise came earlier but were accelerated as civilian agencies began addressing dual-use technology concerns. For example, Japan's first National Security Strategy, released in 2013, called for Japan to promote and develop dual-use technology as the foundation of the country's 'economic strength and defense forces' and emphasised the need to 'make effective use of technology in the areas of security, by combining the efforts of industries, academia, and the Government'.[118] Japan's defence strategy, the National Defense Program Guidelines for fiscal years 2014/15–18/19, updated at the same time with the National Security Strategy in 2013, stated the necessity of using civilian technologies for defence. MOD published its first mid- to long-term defence technology strategy in 2016, with a view to setting the course for Japan's military technology development for the next two decades and to fostering greater interaction with the civilian and, particularly, commercial sectors, and established the Acquisition, Technology & Logistics Agency (ATLA) in 2015 for the purpose of pursuing these goals.[119] Increasing mentions of China's military–civil fusion and civilian technology's spill-over into the military domains in MOD's annual 'Defense of Japan' white papers since 2018 and the first-ever mention of China's military–civil fusion in the 'National Defense Program Guidelines for FY 2019 and beyond' implicitly emphasise that Tokyo's enhanced interaction between Japan's civilian and military sectors is aimed at dealing with the new challenges posed by China.[120]

The three geo-economic goals – FOIP, economic security and military–civil interaction – converged during the course of the second Abe administration. In April 2020, an economic division was created within the NSS to coordinate diplomatic, economic and security interests, providing further evidence of the Abe administration's efforts to adopt an integrated approach at the top levels of government to the geo-economic challenges arising from the economic and military rise of China.

Image 1: **Prime minister Yoshida Shigeru**

(Bettmann via Getty Images)

Image 2: **Deng Xiaoping with prime minister Fukuda Takeo during Deng's visit to Tokyo in October 1978**

(Kurita KAKU via Getty Images)

Image 3: **Prime minister Tanaka Kakuei's visit to China in September 1972**

(Bettmann via Getty Images)

Image 4: **Prime minister Hashimoto Ryutaro on the election campaign in October 1996**

(Noboru Hashimoto via Getty Images)

Image 5: **Prime minister Nakasone Yasuhiro and US president Ronald Reagan at Camp David on 13 April 1986**

(Historical via Getty Images)

Image 6: **Prime minister Koizumi Junichiro campaigning ahead of the September 2005 general election**

(Koichi Kamoshida via Getty Images)

Image 7: **Prime minister Abe Shinzo hosts the 42nd G7 summit at Ise-Shima in May 2016**

(Kurita KAKU via Getty Images)

CHAPTER TWO

Japan's geo-economic strategy: the means

For much of the period since 1945, Japanese economic statecraft – and from the 1970s, its emerging geo-economic strategy – were narrowly focused in terms of both tools and geography. Although Japanese policy was broadly aimed at supporting the US-led international order, it also displayed a strong preference for bilateralism over multilateralism. In comparison with Europe, multilateralism and regionalism have put down only shallow roots in Asia and are largely centred around ASEAN, both formally and informally.[1] The slowness of regional institutions to develop has largely reflected the geopolitics of the region, notably the hub-and-spokes format of US security alliances in the region (which contrasts with the United States' role in the multilateral NATO alliance in Europe); the fact that until the rapid economic rise of China from the early 2000s, the economic focus of much of the region was on the US market rather than on the less-developed and smaller local markets; concerns among US allies in Asia that growth in multilateralism could dilute America's commitment to the region; and fears about the potential for Japan to take a dominant role in regional organisations given the memories of its brutal occupation of many Asian countries and its over-whelming economic preponderance across the region.

Early bilateralism and a strong regional focus

Given this environment and the legal and political constraints on Japan's exercise of hard power, one of the most important policy tools available to Japan has been bilateral ODA.[2] Tokyo's ODA disbursements started in the 1950s and grew steadily in tandem with Japan's increasing weight in the global economy. By 1970, Japan had become the world's fifth-largest ODA donor in US dollar terms, and by 1989 was the largest. During the 1990s, Japan remained either the world's largest or second-largest supplier of such assistance.[3] Despite pressures for spending restraint owing to its poor fiscal position, Tokyo remains one of the world's most important ODA donors, with the overwhelming bulk of its assistance being provided bilaterally.[4] Similar to the criticism levelled at China for its lending under its BRI, the 'quality' of Japan's ODA has been accused of being too closely 'tied' to creating business for Japanese firms in Asia and thus designed to integrate the region more closely with the Japanese economy.[5]

In the early post-war years, Japanese ODA was deployed as a means of rebuilding relations with Asian countries, which had borne the brunt of Japanese militarism in the run-up to, and during, the Second World War. Southeast Asia was a particular focus, which made strategic sense for Japan in view of the region's abundant natural resources – which Japan needed for its own rapid industrial expansion – and because of an imperative to secure access for Japanese goods and investment to the region's growing domestic markets. Japanese economic support for Southeast Asian countries was also intended to supplement US-led efforts to hold back the spread of communism in the region, particularly in the late 1970s after the US defeat in Vietnam. On the back of

Figure 6: **Japanese official development assistance trends, 1965–2017**

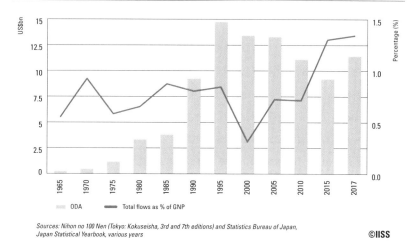

Sources: Nihon no 100 Nen (Tokyo: Kokuseisha, 3rd and 7th editions) and Statistics Bureau of Japan,
Japan Statistical Yearbook, various years   ©IISS

the Fukuda Doctrine, Japanese ODA flows doubled between 1978 and 1980 in cash terms.[6] The Asian focus of Japan's ODA policy was also consistent with its 'flying geese paradigm' (*ganko keitai*) of its economic role in the region, with Japan as the leading, most industrially advanced bird in a V-shaped formation of the region's economies.[7] As late as 1970, Asia was still the destination for an overwhelming 98% of Japanese ODA. Although Asia's share of Japanese ODA lessened as Japan's global economic interests grew in the 1980s and 1990s, the region still accounted for nearly 60% of total disbursements in 1990 and has since remained the largest single regional destination.[8]

Japan's ODA and broader economic focus on Southeast Asia deepened its economic links with the region. By 1972, Japan's share of the region's trade had risen to 32% from just 9% in 1958.[9] These links deepened further from the mid-1980s with the yen's turbo charged appreciation after the Plaza Accord, triggering a rapid increase in Japanese companies' direct investment into the region, particularly the four largest Southeast Asian economies: Indonesia, Malaysia, the Philippines and Thailand.[10] Japanese direct investment into the region picked up again as

Figure 7: **Japanese foreign-direct-investment trends, 1965–2020**

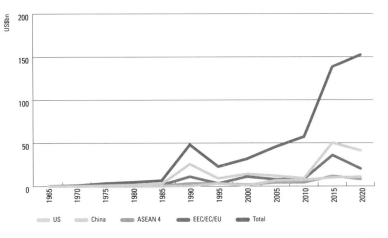

Note: ASEAN 4 denotes Indonesia, Malaysia, the Philippines and Thailand
Source: Japan External Trade Organization

©IISS

the yen's appreciation accelerated in the 1990s, particularly in 1995–96, following renewed US pressure on Japan from 1993–95 to allow its currency to appreciate in order to ease bilateral trade tensions.[11] Japanese electronics, machinery and automotive companies provided the bulk of these investment flows, contributing to the region's industrialisation and its movement up the value chain. Japan remains one of the largest investors and lenders in Southeast Asia, and this has supported the resilience of Japanese influence in the region, even in the face of China's strategic focus on Southeast Asia via its BRI.

From Tokyo's point of view, Japanese ODA to China was a strategic tool for integrating Beijing into the region's broader economy and thus to 'maintain and strengthen the security and prosperity of Japan'.[12] In 1979, Japan agreed to start ODA disbursements to Beijing, which had previously declined foreign aid but reversed course with Deng Xiaoping's initiation of an economic modernisation programme, and the first disbursement agreement was signed in December 1980. Japan thus became the first non-communist country to provide such

Figure 8: **Average US dollar/yen foreign-exchange spot rate, 1971–89**

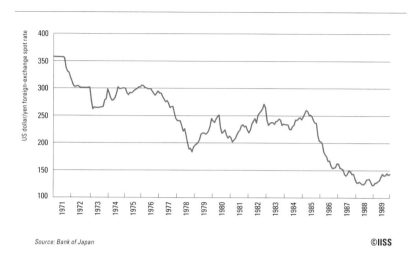

Source: Bank of Japan   ©IISS

aid to Beijing. Tokyo was also eventually to become Beijing's largest source of foreign concessional aid – between 1979 and 2007 when its low-interest loan programme for China ended, Japan's Overseas Economic Cooperation Fund lent some ¥2.5 trillion to China, or around US$25bn at 2007 exchange rates.[13] Japanese financial assistance was thus a critical source of funds for China's economic development. Indeed, between 1979 and the late 1980s Japan provided more than half of the total development loans made by all countries to China.[14] China's reliance on Japanese funds and technology was recognised by Deng. In conversation with Japanese prime minister Nakasone Yasuhiro in March 1984, he said:

> The historical and friendly relations between Japan and China must continue onto the 21st century, and then to the 22nd, 23rd, 33rd, and 43rd century. Currently, Japan and China does [sic] not have urgent problems. The development of Japan–China relations into the 21st century is more important than all other issues.[15]

Figure 9: **Japanese inward investment into China, 1987–2019**

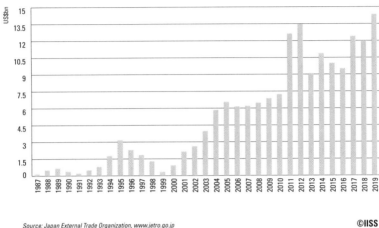

Source: Japan External Trade Organization, www.jetro.go.jp   ©IISS

From the 1980s, Japanese companies were also early investors in China's expanding economy. Investments were, however, mainly concentrated in the electronics sector where Japanese firms were attracted by lower production costs rather than, at this stage, the Chinese market itself, and the services sectors where, for example, transactions were in hard currency and exchange-rate risk was lower. Japanese heavy industry, meanwhile, remained reluctant to invest, reflecting, inter alia, poor infrastructure and regulatory barriers.[16]

Japan's economic rapprochement with China was underpinned by the pragmatic so-called *seikei bunri* principle, under which both sides in effect agreed to keep economic interests and political differences separate.[17] This had already been an important tool for Tokyo in navigating its relations between China and Taiwan after Japan's signing of a peace treaty with Taiwan in 1951.[18] Deng's successful visit to Japan in October 1978, the first by a Chinese leader, and his glimpses of Japanese technology on the tours of Japanese factories and infrastructure during the visit reinforced this pragmatism from the Chinese side and its willingness to let 'bygones be bygones' in the interests of strengthening bilateral relations.[19] Japanese investment in China helped to boost bilateral trade, and by 1985 Japan had become China's biggest trading partner.[20] Tokyo ended its lending programme to China in 2018, arguing, not unreasonably, that Japanese aid was no longer needed given that China's economy had overtaken Japan's in terms of size in 2010.[21]

Multilateralism: a mixed record

Japan's desire to exert economic and political influence in Asia through multilateral mechanisms grew in line with its rising global economic importance. One of Tokyo's early successes in this respect came in 1966 with the establishment of the ADB, the first multilateral institution that Japan had created and led, which was intended to fund development projects in the region. Japan provided the first president of the ADB, Watanabe Takeshi, and every president since. ASEAN, set up in 1967, also became an important channel for Japanese engagement in the region, despite occasional strains arising from Southeast Asian perceptions of predatory economic behaviour by Japan: concerns over Japan's 'economic imperialism' were a trigger for the boycotting of Japanese goods and anti-Japanese riots during prime minister Tanaka Kakuei's visit to Thailand and Indonesia in 1974.[22]

The announcement in 1977 by Tanaka's successor but one as prime minister, Fukuda Takeo, of more balanced Japanese 'heart to heart' engagement with the region that included political, social and cultural as well as economic dimensions, encapsulated in the so-called Fukuda Doctrine, was intended to reset Japan's relations with the region as well as to buttress a regional order destabilised by the advance of communism in Cambodia, Laos and Vietnam. This led to three Japan–ASEAN dialogue bodies being established in the late 1970s.[23] Tokyo was also an early agitator for what in 1994 became the ASEAN Regional Forum (ARF): in July 1991 Japanese foreign minister Nakayama Taro floated the idea of an Asian security forum in the form of a senior officials' meeting that would report to the ASEAN Post-Ministerial Conference.[24] Although the ARF has subsequently disappointed many observers by failing to play an active role in managing the region's security challenges, at the time its establishment appeared to be a significant development for the region's multilateral frameworks in that the formal initiative was undertaken by ASEAN rather than by one of the major regional powers.[25] The first-ever meeting between the Japanese and North Korean foreign ministers, Kono Yohei and Paek Nam Sun respectively, was held at the ARF in July 2000.[26]

Japan's experience of wielding multilateral tools was, however, mixed. Its lead role together with Australia in the creation of the APEC forum in 1989 was an important initiative designed to promote regional economic integration through trade liberalisation and 'open regionalism'.[27] APEC would also deliver a political dividend for Japan and the region in binding the US and China (which joined in 1991, along with Taiwan and Hong Kong) more tightly into the regional order while offering smaller countries a forum in which they would not be forced to choose between either the US or China. APEC was also in part defensive, 'born out of fear', reflecting Tokyo's concerns about global trade fragmentation following the signing in 1986 of the Single European Act, which aimed to create a single market in the European Community (now the European Union) by 1992, and the conclusion of the North Atlantic Free Trade Agreement (NAFTA) by Canada, Mexico and the US in 1988.[28]

But APEC's progress in the 1990s foundered. China, concerned that APEC might become a tool for increasing US influence in the region, agitated from the start to weaken the grouping's institutionalisation.[29] The Asian financial and economic crises in 1997–98, coupled with the difficulties of Japan's own post-bubble-collapse economic adjustment, undercut international confidence in the 'Asian economic model', while in 1998 domestic pressure from the then-powerful domestic agricultural lobby persuaded the Japanese government to refuse to endorse so-called early voluntary sector liberalisation (EVSL), a package of tariff-reduction measures by APEC members on agricultural products.[30] Japan led broader opposition to EVSL within APEC, thus derailing the organisation's long-term liberalisation schedule. China's spectacular economic rise after its accession to the WTO in 2001 and the broader retreat from globalisation after the 2008 global financial crisis were further headwinds for APEC in the 2000s. Japan's own switch to a bilateral free-trade agreement (FTA) strategy in the 2000s, reflecting the gridlocking of the WTO's Doha trade round, and starting in 2002 with the Japan–Singapore FTA, further undercut APEC's momentum.

Japan's attempts to create an Asia-only multilateral AMF in 1997 to coordinate the region's response to the Asian financial crisis – and to protect its own significant investments – was one of Tokyo's periodic attempts to increase Japan's influence in the region.[31] The effort failed, however, owing to opposition from the US and others concerned that the AMF would compete with and thus potentially undermine the US-led IMF and the 'Washington Consensus'.[32] China, which in an early display of its own geo-economic power had indicated that it would not devalue its currency and aggravate the regional financial crisis, was also reluctant to join.[33] Japan's initial 'low posture' approach to the AMF proposal was unhelpful in terms of rallying support for the initiative; instead, Tokyo asked Thailand to be the public face of the plan and to propose the idea.[34] Had it been able to function, given Japan's heavy economic exposure to Southeast Asia, a Japanese AMF is unlikely to have insisted on the strict conditionality that marked the initial phase of the IMF regional bailout in late 1997 and early 1998 and which deepened the economic downturns of the worst-affected countries. Japanese support for Malaysia's September 1998 capital controls, which the IMF opposed, also points to potential for policy conflict with a Japanese-led AMF.[35]

Japan enjoyed better fortunes with its New Miyazawa Initiative, which followed in October 1998, perhaps partly reflecting more assiduous courting of the US and China than had been the case with the AMF.[36] The initiative proposed creating a liquidity fund to act as a bulwark against future financial crises in the region and, following this, Japan signed bilateral currency swap arrangements with Malaysia and South Korea.[37] These formed the basis of the CMI currency swap arrangement established in May 2000 between the ten ASEAN member states and Japan, China and South Korea, the 'ASEAN + 3'. As well as emergency financing, the initiative also aimed to promote the ability of the ASEAN + 3 to track and share 'consistent and timely data and information on capital flows'.[38] The CMI was upgraded in March 2010 to create the Chiang Mai Initiative Multilateralization (CMIM), and in 2020 coordination between the CMIM and the IMF was tightened.[39] To date, however, neither the resources of the CMI nor those of the CMIM have been deployed, partly reflecting the substantial liquidity buffers built up since the 1997–98 Asian financial and economic crises by the crisis countries and others in the region.

The 1997–98 crises also created fresh impetus for Japan to exert its economic influence to stabilise regional currencies. Tokyo tried to do this in April 1999 with the renewed policy push to internationalise the yen.[40] The idea was that the yen would serve as an anchor for the region's other currencies, reducing the 'over-dependence on the US dollar' that in the Japanese government's view had been one of the causes of the financial and economic turbulence of 1997–98.[41] Internationalisation would also ensure that the yen's role was 'commensurate with the share of the Japanese economy in the world and Japan's status as the world's largest net creditor nation'.[42] The looming launch of the euro and its potential role as challenger to US dollar dominance was a further spur to action in Tokyo. A bigger global role for the yen might also make the Japanese currency less volatile, particularly against many Asian currencies given Japan's close economic ties with the region – during the 1990s the yen had veered from extreme appreciation in the middle of the decade, reaching a post-Second World War nominal high of around ¥80:US$1 in mid-1995, to near collapse in mid-1998, falling below ¥140:US$1, and rallying to around ¥100:US$1 by the end of 1999.[43]

The policy failed, however, to lift global yen use significantly and, by 2003, Japanese government momentum behind the policy was already ebbing.[44] Lack of success for Tokyo reflected continued uncertainty about the trajectory of Japan's economy, particularly given the weakness of its banks and the need for greater reform of its own capital markets. The shift of the region's economic centre of gravity to China after its WTO accession in 2001 was a further obstacle to Japanese attempts to increase yen use. Indeed, Beijing also subsequently came to attach strategic importance to the internationalisation of its currency, the renminbi, although this was more explicitly directed at reducing US dollar dominance.[45]

Japan was a founding member in 1975 of the G7 leading industrialised democracies and a member of its predecessor, the more informal G5. The G7 has in theory been an important forum for Japan to exert influence on global governance, particularly given its status as the sole Asian member. In practice, however, with few exceptions, Japan's ability to project influence, geo-economic or otherwise, via the G5 and later the G7 has proved weaker than policymakers in Tokyo might have liked. In part, this has reflected Japan's deference to the US, for example, in the 1975 Plaza Accord. Another reason was Japan's own economic malaise in the 1990s following the collapse of its bubble economy, which set in while most other G7 economies were performing strongly and sapped Japanese policy credibility, particularly on the economic front. Relatedly, except under Koizumi Junichiro's 2001–06 administration or Abe Shinzo's from 2012–20, Japan's ability to conduct personal diplomacy at the G7 has been constrained by the high turnover of prime ministers – there were, for example, 15 between 1990 and 2012.

As the G7's only Asian power, Japan has also struggled to secure alignment of this grouping, dominated as it is by North Americans and Western Europeans, with some of its foreign- policy initiatives. Tokyo's attempt to internationalise its Northern Territories/Kuriles territorial dispute with Russia in the 1990s via the G7 is a good example of this.[46] Japan was unable to secure consistent G7 support for its hard line, which included the threat of withholding economic aid for Russia's beleaguered post-communist economy.[47] Japan had thus failed to read the shifting geopolitical priorities of its G7 peers following the collapse of the Soviet Union. Since the 2000s, the rise of China and other large emerging markets, and the relative decline of US power, have weakened the influence of the G7. The formation of the G20 at the time of the 2008 global financial crisis, which includes China and other large emerging markets such as Brazil, India and Russia, only underscored the G7's eclipse as a forum for global influence, with many decisions taken by the G7 having limited viability unless also supported by the G20.

Internal balancing under Abe 2.0: economics, institutions and capabilities

Abe Shinzo's second administration marked a structural break with its predecessors in terms of geo-economic strategy in four main ways: the range of tools deployed; the focus of Japanese economic statecraft on building norms as well as on supporting the international rules-based order; the overlap of these tools with Japan's broader evolving security policy; and the strategy of building international coalitions of the 'like-minded' (*dōshikoku*) in order to amplify and buttress Japanese policy. In the round, the geo-economic means adopted under Abe's second administration reflected a strong emphasis on boosting Japanese 'agency through convening power', itself part of an ideologically motivated drive by Abe to restore Japanese policy autonomy lost in the post-1945 settlement.[48] The impact of the rapid growth of Chinese economic and political power from the early 2000s provided an additional impetus for Abe's push to accelerate Japan's evolution as a global power, not least his desire to engage China from a position of strength.

A distinguishing feature of the policy platform of Abe's second administration was the focus on restoring Japanese economic health.[49] Central to this was the economic programme known as 'Abenomics', consisting of three so-called 'arrows': ultra-loose monetary policy, which would end Japan's prolonged deflation; flexible deployment of fiscal policy, which would support growth while not aggravating Japan's weak public finances; and productivity-enhancing structural reforms. The first arrow was the most innovative, with the Bank of Japan (BOJ, the central bank) introducing new targets and timelines for re-igniting consumer-price inflation, ramping up asset purchases in order to boost liquidity in the Japanese economy, and introducing negative interest rates and caps on 10-year Japanese government bond yields. With these measures, the BOJ signalled a structural break with its previous policy reticence. This in turn resulted in a steady weakening of the yen against the US dollar from an average of around ¥100 in 2013 to ¥106 in 2014 and ¥120 in 2015, providing useful support to Japanese growth.[50] Although the BOJ consistently failed to reach its official inflation target, it appears to have ended Japan's persistent deflation. The fact that even after Abe's departure from office in 2020 there have been no serious challenges to continuing the policy underscores its success in changing domestic policy perceptions.

The fiscal and structural reform arrows of 'Abenomics' were less successful. Notwithstanding the fiscal loosening early in his second premiership, Abe also implemented two consumption-tax increases, one in April 2014, raising the tax from 5% to 8%, and another in October 2019, increasing the tax to 10%, although this second increase was twice delayed from the original April 2017 target. It is a measure of Abe's political dominance that he was able to preside over two such increases in this unpopular tax which had contributed to the downfall of two previous prime ministers: Takeshita Noboru in 1989 and Hashimoto Ryutaro in 1998.[51] Abe's decision to raise the consumption-tax made sense from a fiscal point of view. Japan has the worst public finances in the developed world, with the gross public debt stock already at 226% of its GDP at end-2012, rising to 234% by end-2019 and, boosted by COVID-19 support measures for the economy, to nearly 260% by end-2020.[52] The fiscal tightening may, however, also have undercut the BOJ's anti-deflation efforts. The timing of the second increase was also highly unfortunate, given its proximity to the 2020 coronavirus pandemic.

Structural reforms are always politically difficult for any government. The lack of progress in Abe's second term was, however, especially striking given its prominence on his policy platform, and may have reflected its low political priority for Abe compared with, say, security reform, where progress was far more rapid. Thus, Abe's structural reforms yielded only modest results, failing to boost Japan's persistently poor productivity.[53] Productivity improvement is vital for the health of Japan's economy if it is to offset the financial and resource impact of its steep demographic decline. Japan's working-age population has been declining since 1996 on the back of stubbornly low fertility rates and its overall population has been falling since its peak in 2009. Meanwhile, increasing longevity has steadily raised the percentage of elderly in the population, with those aged 65 and over accounting for nearly 30% of the total in 2020.[54] The impact of this imbalance between old and young in Japan is evident in the dramatic shifts in Japan's potential support ratios. In 1950, Japan had around 12 working-age people (aged 15–64) to support each person aged 65 and over; by 2050, this will have fallen to around one working-age person for each elderly person.[55]

The need for productivity improvement is particularly acute in Japan's vast small and medium-sized enterprise (SME) sector, whose firms have long been coddled by generous government support. Many of the owners of these firms are also ageing. OECD data suggests that two-thirds of this cohort will be aged 70 and over by 2025.[56] In 2018, according to the government white paper on SMEs, the sector accounted for 99.7% of all Japanese firms – of which 14.8% were medium-sized enterprises and 84.9% small firms – and employed around 70% of the private-sector labour force. The dominance in terms of numbers and employment of Japan's SMEs was not, however, reflected in their value added to the economy. According to the same white paper, this stood at 14% for small firms, 38.9% for medium-sized firms and 47.1% for the largest firms.[57] Weakness in Japan's SMEs thus remains an Achilles' heel for Japan's economic health and its economic security too.

Abe complemented his economic reforms with brisk implementation of a series of far-reaching security reforms. Like his post-Cold War predecessors, Abe initiated these partly in response to external pressure, specifically China's rise. But Abe's security-policy changes tried not only to widen the scope of Japan's defence cooperation with the US and its regional partners through greater inter-operability, but also to change how Japan conceptualised its security policy. The latter point was evident in the promulgation of Japan's first-ever National Security Strategy and the establishment of a National Security Council (NSC), both in December 2013, and in the setting up of a coordinating body for the NSC, the NSS, in January 2014. Abe had tried to establish an NSC during his first premiership, but momentum behind the idea stalled after he left office in September 2007.

The NSC is one of Abe's most important security reforms and among the most important of Japan's post-Second World War institutional changes. Designed to improve the intra-governmental coordination of Japan's foreign and security policy, establishing the NSC also meant that for the first time since 1945 Japan's Cabinet Secretariat had a unified foreign and security policy 'control tower' (*shireitō*), thus strengthening prime-ministerial control over these key policy areas.[58] Its establishment also recognised the need for Japan to deal with threats to national security across a broad front, one that subsumes challenges from emerging technologies, relatively new domains such as cyber, and economic coercion. In addition, the cabinet-level NSC mirrors its US counterpart with a view to improving alliance coordination.

As part of its 'control' function, the NSC seeks to improve policy efficiency by introducing a hierarchy of meetings, the most important of which is the Four-minister Meeting

Figure 10: **Number of NSC meetings held annually, 2013–21**

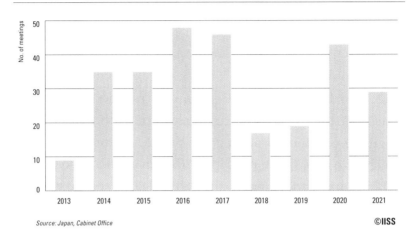

Source: Japan, Cabinet Office   ©IISS

attended by the prime minister, who chairs the meeting, the foreign affairs minister, the defence minister and the chief cabinet secretary (*Yon Daijin Kaigō*). This meeting, which may, if conditions require, take place weekly, sets broad foreign and security goals. This is supported by the Nine-minister Meeting (*Kyū Daijin Kaigō*), which includes the four core ministers plus the ministers of finance, economy, trade and industry, land, infrastructure and transport, public management, home affairs, posts and telecommunications, and the national security advisor. A third type of meeting is convened in the event of national-security emergencies (*Kinkyū Jitai Daijin Kaigō*) and includes the prime minister, the chief cabinet secretary and others as needed.[59]

The NSC's predecessor, the Security Council (SC), had been established by prime minister Nakasone Yasuhiro in July 1986, but it met only infrequently during its nearly 30 years of existence, while policymaking efficiency was undermined by its reliance on revolving secondments to its secretariat from various ministries.[60] The SC was mainly concerned with SDF deployment and budgetary issues so, unsurprisingly, it failed

Figure 11: **Japan's NSC meetings, by category, 2013–21**

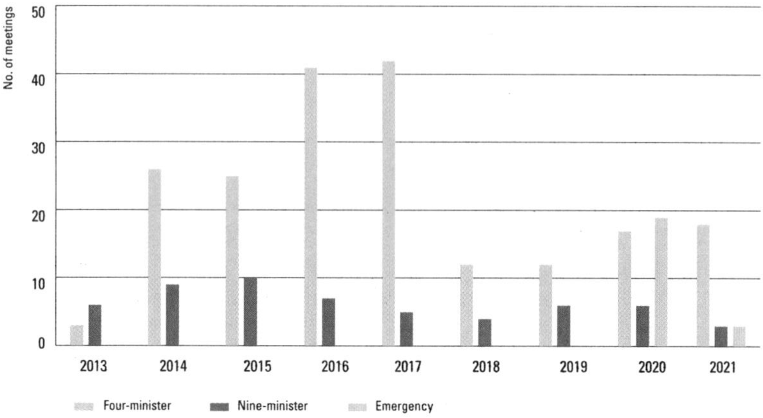

Note: 2021 data is until 1 December
Source: Japan, Cabinet Office

©IISS

to evolve into a forum for developing long-term national-security strategy or for linking this with foreign policy. Unlike the NSC, the SC only met on an ad hoc basis to discuss specific issues. The SC's format was also more unwieldy than that of the NSC, consisting only of the organisationally more cumbersome Nine-minister Meeting, which was retained in the NSC.

Given the fragmented state of Japan's bureaucracy, the NSS's coordinating function gives it a critical supporting role for the NSC. One core function of the NSS is to gather information from across government under the so-called 'DIME' (diplomatic–informational–military–economic) framework for input into responses to the requests for analysis handed down by the NSC. The Secretariat has formal authority from the prime minister to do this, and to reinforce its political authority, its secretary-general reports directly to the prime minister. Evidence suggests that it has been at least moderately successful in forcing information to be shared across agencies.[61] However, in relation to the breadth of its coverage, the NSS is thinly resourced and its staff of around 100, drawn from across Japan's ministries and includ-

Figure 12: **Frequency of topics discussed at Japan's NSC, 2013–21**

Topics discussed at NSC meetings (2013–21)	Frequency	Note
Issues on North Korea	56	North Korea's ballistic-missile launches (40); situation in North Korea (13); nuclear tests (2); situation on the Korean Peninsula (1).
COVID-19 response	24	
Issues on Japan's peacekeeping operation (PKO)	23	Including Japan's PKO in South Sudan and the Sinai Peninsula and Japan's mission to protect US equipment in the PKO.
South Sudan (regional situation and Japan's PKO activity)	22	PKO in South Sudan (18).
Situations in the Indo-Pacific region	22	First use of the Indo-Pacific was in April 2017; last use of 'Asia-Pacific' and 'South Asia' in 2016 (11 times on Asia-Pacific and three times on South Asia); last use of 'Asia' in 2014.
Situations in East Asia	19	Mentioned the situation around the Senkaku/Diaoyu islands in 2021 (2).
Situations in the Middle East	18	Japan's PKO on the Sinai Peninsula (4) and in Afghanistan (1); security of Japan-related vessels in the Middle East.
Military build-up	10	
Prime minister's approval of anti-piracy operations	9	
Various security issues for Japan	8	
Situation in Ukraine	7	All meetings were held in 2014.
Japan's response to ballistic-missile threats	8	Six meetings held after the cancellation of the *Aegis Ashore* system in June 2020.
Maritime security	6	
Review of the National Defense Program Guidelines (NDPG)	5	
Security environment in cyberspace	5	

Sources: IISS; Japan, Cabinet Office

ing officers from the National Police Agency, the Maritime Safety Agency and the SDF, is small compared with that of some other countries' equivalent agencies.[62]

In 2013, Abe drove through the passage of a Designated State Secrets Law (DSSL), which created the Japanese government's first document classification system to protect state secrets and facilitate the exchange of military intelligence and defence-industrial data with the US and close security partners such as Australia and the UK.[63] The legislation was also designed to bring some order to Japan's siloed intelligence-gathering-related protocols. For Japan, the introduction of the DSSL was a radical move given the post-1945 constraints: the country's intelligence capabilities were emasculated after the war as part of the initial demilitarisation under the Allied occupation. During the Cold War, the strengthening of Japan's indigenous intelligence-gathering capabilities was hampered by the US: Washington was even reported to have blocked Tokyo's acquisition of surveillance satellites,[64] and significant constitutional and legal constraints on the rebuilding of these capabilities still remain today.[65] As with much of Japan's security debate, discussion of intelligence matters is politically charged, particularly given its link with Japan's pre-war militarism. However, the DSSL was only the first step towards the reforms needed to reinforce Japan's ability to gather and share intelligence.

Three further significant security-related reforms accompanied the changes to the domestic security framework. The first came in July 2014 with Cabinet approval for a reinterpretation of the constitution to allow Japan to exercise the right of 'collective self-defence' under certain conditions to support US operations in the region. The second reform was a revision in April 2015 to the US–Japan Guidelines for Defence Cooperation, the first since 1997. The revised Guidelines expanded the scope of US–Japan security cooperation considerably by emphasising 'the global nature of the Japan–US Alliance'; widening the scope under which Japan could use force to include responding to attacks 'against the United States or a third country'; widening the geographical scope for Japan to provide rear-area support for US forces from the 'areas surrounding Japan' for the first time since 1997 to include areas such as the Taiwan Strait; and introducing the concept of 'grey zone contingencies' necessitating 'seamless' responses 'under any circumstances, from peacetime to contingencies'; and stressing the importance for Japan's security of the 'space and cyberspace domains'.[66] The third reform was the passage of legislation in September 2015 to expand the scope of SDF activities by enabling 'collective self-defence' in contingencies where Japan's survival was threatened and to enable implementation of the revised US–Japan Guidelines for Defence Cooperation.

Abe's ability to initiate reforms at this pace owed much to earlier electoral and administrative reforms, notably the shift from multiple to single MPs for parliamentary constituencies (starting with the 1996 general election), and the large-scale reorganisation of Japan's ministries (implemented in 2001). Both these changes shifted power away from vested interests in the LDP to the prime minister. Together with Abe's launch in 2014 of the Cabinet Bureau of Personnel Affairs to control key civil-service appointments, they helped to consolidate prime-ministerial authority further during Abe's long second administration.

From around 2018, Tokyo focused its internal balancing increasingly on economic security issues in order to bolster economic resilience. One important move was the expansion of the NSS in April 2020 to include a new economics unit, designed to serve as the central command to coordinate and craft economic security policies.[67] Although small, with only around 20 staff, the unit is nevertheless the Secretariat's largest single unit. The range of subjects handled by the NSS economics team is broad, including protection of intellectual property, digital currencies, supply-chain resilience and 5G, thus reflecting Japan's concerns about Chinese activity in these areas. The economics unit is also tasked with boosting Japanese representation in international organisations. Japan has been lagging behind China in terms of occupying senior positions in international institutions. Beijing has actively strengthened its representation at these institutions, viewing them as important vehicles for boosting its influence over global standards, particularly in new technology sectors where in many cases the rules have yet to be formulated. As of mid-2021, China held the top positions at four of the 15 specialised agencies of the UN, while Japan held none; between end-2015 and end-2019, the numbers of Japanese working at international institutions rose by 23%, against an increase of 42% in Chinese representation.[68]

Tokyo has also taken important steps to strengthen defensive measures aimed at preventing outflow of sensitive technologies and information as a result of foreign direct investment. For example, in April 2020 Tokyo revised the Japanese Foreign Exchange and Foreign Trade Act to tighten foreign-investment screening, and lowered the threshold beyond which regulatory approval was necessary from 10% to 1% foreign ownership.[69] In June 2021, the Diet passed legislation that allows the government to use the investment-screening mechanism to scrutinise real-estate ownership and the use of land in order to prevent foreign entities and individuals from buying land or property that could be sensitive from a national-security viewpoint.[70] By 2021, Tokyo was also reportedly considering introducing regulations on foreign equipment in 14 critical infrastructure sectors, including telecommunications, electricity and transportation, to enhance cybersecurity.[71] METI was also considering tighter regulations on foreign students accessing research laboratories to prevent technology outflow from Japan.[72]

Japan's government also took measures, particularly from 2018, to enhance Japan's competitiveness in advanced technologies in which China had made significant advances.[73] One example was support for the development and marketing overseas of Japanese telecommunications equipment that could provide alternatives to Chinese 5G systems. To this end, during 2020 the Diet passed legislation that provided tax credits to Japanese telecommunications suppliers developing 5G systems and drones with open standards that do not require vendor lock-in.[74] Beneficiaries were intended to include suppliers of Open Radio Access Network (RAN) 5G, a network system that disaggregates hardware and software components of 5G networks. Open RAN is a multi-vendor system, unlike current architecture, which is dominated by a few players, including most notably China's Huawei, China's largest telecommunications company. To boost the international competitiveness of Japan's basic research, the 5th Science, Technology, and Innovation Basic Plan, the five-year technology strategy put together by the Cabinet's Council for Science, Technology and Innovation (CSTI) adopted in March 2021, directed, among other things, the government to set up a ¥10trn (US$96bn) fund by March 2022 for Japanese universities.[75]

Efforts to boost the competitiveness of advanced dual-use technology also came from MOD's defence-equipment procurement body, the Acquisition, Technology and Logistics Agency (ATLA), established in 2015. ATLA emerged from the Medium Term Defense Program (MTDP) for fiscal years 2014/15 to 2018/19 and was intended to improve coordination across MOD's divisions and the three services in defence R&D, procurement and equipment-export activities, with the latter taking advantage of the loosening of legal restrictions on such exports in 2014. Thus, ATLA's creation recognised both the weakness of Japan's indigenous defence industry in the face of competition from British, French and US companies and the need to boost Japan's own defence-technology base in the face of fierce competition from China in areas such as cyber, the electromagnetic spectrum, AI and hypersonics. In 2015–16, ATLA set up a new funding mechanism, the National Security Technology Research Promotion Fund, to promote basic research in advanced technology areas with potential military use. To expand the scope and accelerate the speed of the R&D programme, the government had increased the size of this fund from the initial ¥600m to ¥11bn by 2021.[76] Tokyo is also reportedly setting up a US$875 million fund outside MOD to accelerate dual-use technology R&D in AI, quantum technology, biotechnology and robotics.[77]

Abe's external balancing: coalition-building with an economic focus

A distinctive feature of the policy framework of Abe's second administration was to complement the strengthening of the domestic economy and national-security frameworks with a broad programme of external balancing, which deployed geo-economic strategy to meet the geo-economic challenge from China. The two core pillars of this external balancing, support for the rules-based order and for building coalitions of the like-minded, were already evident in Abe's first administration in 2006–07. For example, in his January 2007 speech to NATO's decision-making body, the North Atlantic Council, the first by a Japanese prime minister, Abe outlined the need for Japan to 'identify the best possible synergies with like-minded partners around the globe' and emphasised 'fundamental values such [as] freedom, democracy, human rights and the rule of law'.[78] In Abe's strategy, these two pillars would be critical to increasing Japanese agency in Asia in order to manage the rise of China as well as the ebbing of US power and, particularly during the 'America first' administration of Donald Trump from 2017–21, its eroding commitment to the region. Coalitions and rules would – Abe intended – help to preserve the regional balance of power, offset Chinese attempts to undermine the rules-based order in Asia, and manage US decline.

The central organising framework for Abe's external-balancing geo-economic strategy was the FOIP concept. While first announced in August 2016,[79] it originated during Abe's first term and the 'Confluence of the Two Seas' speech that he delivered to the Indian parliament in New Delhi in 2007, during the course of which he highlighted the 'dynamic coupling as seas of freedom and prosperity' of the Pacific and Indian oceans.[80] The choice of location for the speech signalled Abe's intent to draw the 'born democracy' and 'future super power' that was India into the international rules-based order in order to balance China's rise.[81] The centrality of the maritime domain to the strategic thinking behind FOIP was evident again early in Abe's second administration in a policy speech intended to be delivered during his visit to Jakarta in January 2013, in which he stressed that 'Japan's national interest lies eternally in keeping Asia's seas unequivocally open, free and peaceful'.[82] In this, Abe was – whether consciously or unconsciously – echoing Kosaka Masataka's conceptualisation of Japan as a 'maritime nation' (*kaiyō kokka*), dependent on the sea for both its prosperity and its security: 'Japan is a maritime nation in that her security is threatened if hostile powers gain control of the surrounding seas, and in that she must live by trade, for which she is suitably located.'[83]

Central to the FOIP strategy are preserving the rule of law and protecting the interests of all the countries in the huge Indo-Pacific region, stretching from East Africa through Asia to the Pacific seaboard of the Americas. Given the great importance of the region's markets and trade routes in the global economy, FOIP resonated well beyond the Indo-Pacific, as demonstrated when countries outside the region such as Germany and the UK themselves subsequently articulated Indo-Pacific policies that subscribed to the 'free and open' formulation. FOIP also created a new framework through which Japan could encourage the US to maintain its focus on the region, particularly in terms of economic cooperation.[84]

FOIP rests on three pillars that link Japan's economic and physical security: promotion of the rule of law, freedom of navigation and free trade; pursuit of economic prosperity by improving economic and institutional connectivity; and a commitment to peace and stability through capacity-building and humanitarian assistance.[85] This drawing together of Japan's economic, foreign and security policies, which had hitherto existed broadly as separate from each other, and the expansion of the range of interlocutors to achieve what the Japanese government calls a 'pro-active contribution to peace' (*sekkyo-kuteki heiwashugi*) makes FOIP a significant departure from previous Japanese statecraft.[86] The scale of Tokyo's ambition for the framework is suggested by the comparison drawn by a former senior member of the Japanese government between FOIP and policies for the US advanced by George Kennan in his 1947 'X' article in *Foreign Affairs*.[87] Kennan's piece argued the case for the US to adopt 'a policy of firm containment, designed to confront the Russians with unalterable counter-force at every point where they show signs of encroaching upon the interests of a peaceful and stable world' and became a core US policy for meeting the strategic challenge from the Soviet Union early in the Cold War.

FOIP emphasises the quality of development undertaken under its auspices as part of its economic rule-making – as Abe noted in his TICAD VI speech: 'there must be nothing other than "quality infrastructure"'.[88] FOIP's principles thus sit in implicit contradistinction to China's BRI which, according to its critics, is opaque, damaging to recipients of Chinese funds, characterised by poor-quality infrastructure and, being Beijing-focused, lacks the synergies of network connectivity. Nevertheless, FOIP is not intended to exclude China.[89] Inclusion within FOIP, however, depends on Beijing accepting the international rules that FOIP embodies. This reflects FOIP's strategy of trying to bind China into the rules-based status quo as well as the economic reality that Japan cannot afford to antagonise its most important market. This theoretical openness to China is also reflected in Japan's openness to working with Beijing on BRI projects, where 'these meet common concepts shared by the international community'.[90] Like the US, however, Japan has neither endorsed the BRI nor joined the Chinese-led but multilateral BRI development entity, the AIIB. As was the case with the reaction of the US and others to Japan's AMF proposal in 1997, Tokyo sees the AIIB as a competitor to existing multilateral institutions, notably the IMF and the World Bank as well as the Japanese-led ADB, and has concerns about the quality of the institution's governance.[91]

The CPTPP mega trade deal, which initially involved 11 countries and around 15% of global trade, was formally launched in December 2018. Japan's was by far the largest economy involved in the Partnership, which was a foreign-policy highlight of Abe's second administration. Keeping negotiations on track following the US decision to withdraw from the CPTPP's predecessor, the TPP, in 2017 was a considerable political achievement for Tokyo. Japan's status as an Asian economy with an 'economic catch-up' history of its own allowed Tokyo to play an effective intermediary role between the less advanced and more advanced economies in the bloc.[92] For Japan it was also a ground-breaking deal that not only 'multilateralised the Pacific's economic architecture', but also marked a strategic shift for Tokyo from seeing trade deals in terms of their potential cost to domestic vested interests (particularly the politically powerful agricultural lobby) to understanding their potential rewards for Japan's economy as a whole.[93]

The damage-limitation approach had been evident in the issue of the EVSLs at APEC, as well as in Tokyo's switch to conclude bilateral FTAs in the 2000s with countries such as Singapore where trade liberalisation would not have a signif-

Figure 13: **Trade agreements in the Indo-Pacific**

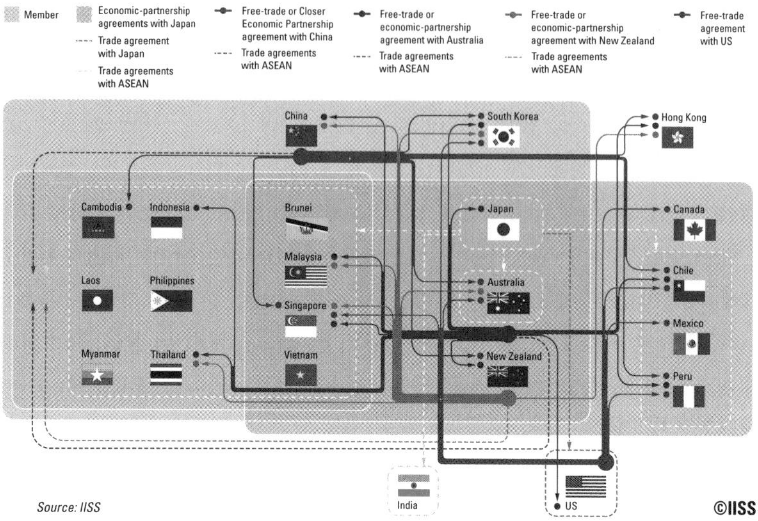

Source: IISS   ©IISS

icant impact on key Japanese vested interests (notably in agriculture), or where Japan was able to exert leverage in order to protect these as in the case of the FTA with Mexico in 2012. Japan's 2015 FTA with Australia was its first with an economy that included a large-scale agricultural sector – the eight years that it took from the initiation of the negotiations in 2007 to their conclusion was a reflection of the strength of the Japanese farming lobby. Abe's willingness in the wake of his landslide victory in the 2012 election in effect to disregard the farming lobby in the TPP/CPTPP negotiations was striking and did much to ensure the successful outcome of the negotiations. His setting up of a special TPP unit, the Government Headquarters for the TPP (*TPP Sōgō Taisaku Honbu*), in the Cabinet Secretariat Office in 2015 to bypass lobbying groups in the various affected ministries, and thereby advance the negotiations, was a sign of the strategic importance that Abe attached to the TPP.[94]

The CPTPP is notable for the high quality of the market liberalisation that it aspires to, as well as its inclusion of a chapter on digital commerce. This is not only consistent with the FOIP concept in terms of quality, but also with Japanese support for the rules-based and open trading order. The emergence of the Chinese-dominated 15-member RCEP mega trade bloc, which was agreed in December 2020 and covers some 30% of global trade, has increased the geopolitical importance of the CPTPP as well as Japan's role: it is the only major power belonging to both regional mega trade blocs as well as being additionally linked into the region through its bilateral FTA network. In many ways, RCEP sits in contradistinction to the CPTPP, as FOIP does to BRI. RCEP's standards are lower than those of the CPTPP, unsurprisingly so given the wide differentials in development levels among its members. Its digital-trade provisions are thin, and agriculture and labour issues are barely touched on. RCEP also has little to say on industrial subsidies or state-owned enterprises, as one would expect given the important role both play in Chinese industrial policy.

Given the gravitational pull of the Chinese economy, however, RCEP is likely to bind the region more closely into Beijing's orbit and act as a tool for Chinese attempts to write economic rules in the region. From Japan's point of view, India's refusal to join RCEP (out of concern for the negative impact of liberalisation on uncompetitive sectors of its economy) will only aggravate this: Tokyo had hoped that India would join Japan as a democratic counterbalance to China in the bloc. However, the CPTPP is already an important counterbalance to RCEP, and Japan's support for the accession of the UK and others reflects Tokyo's need to sustain its momentum in the face of the RCEP challenge.[95] In September 2021 Beijing applied to join the CPTPP.[96] The tough conditionality of the CPTPP suggests, however, that Chinese accession is unlikely in the short term.[97] But, as with FOIP, Tokyo is likely to remain open in principle to

China's joining even though it will be reluctant to agree to relax CPTPP standards in order to allow this to happen.

The CPTPP's geopolitical potential is already evident as the bloc shows signs of evolving beyond trade into economic security. The example of Chile's award of a contract to run an undersea cable to Asia to the Japanese company NEC, one of the world's largest suppliers of submarine cables, in preference to Huawei, illustrates this well. NEC's bid envisaged running the cable from Chile to New Zealand and then to Australia, thus keeping the data flow within the 'like-minded' CPTPP community. Huawei's cable, meanwhile, would have made landfall in Shanghai. Undersea cables have considerable strategic importance given increasing cross-border data flows.[98] One observer has described them, together with 5G, as the 'oil pipelines of the 21st century' just as data is the new oil.[99] The US-led push to 'decouple' supply chains in strategic sectors such as semiconductors from China enhances the CPTPP's importance as a rules-based alternative to locating production in China.

Abe's securing of support for what is in effect FOIP's second pillar – 'economic connectivity' – at the June 2019 G20 summit in Osaka was another important example of Japanese coalition-building in support of Japanese economic statecraft and rule-making. The backing took the form of the grouping's endorsement of the 'G20 Principles for Quality Infrastructure Investment'.[100] China's acquiescence may have reflected a desire by Beijing to improve relations with Tokyo in the face of a sharp deterioration in Sino-US relations as well as to deflect international criticism of the BRI. But President Xi's speech at the November 2020 APEC CEO Dialogues, in which he called for China 'to pursue high-quality Belt and Road cooperation with its partners', was consistent with the Osaka G20 QII principles.[101] As a coda to these principles, in September 2019 the EU and Japan agreed to support sustainable connectivity and quality infrastructure and in November 2019, on the sidelines of the ASEAN summit, Australia, Japan and the US announced the 'Blue Dot Network', an international certification scheme for high-quality infrastructure projects.[102]

Abe's desire for Japan to play a role in shaping global economic governance was also evident in his setting up of the 'Osaka Track' on the sidelines of the 2019 G20 summit to secure rules for the protection of open cross-border data flows – the so-called DFFT. Originally an idea floated by Abe in a speech at the January 2019 World Economic Forum meeting in Davos-Klosters, the 'Osaka Track' DFFT initiative was born out of a recognition that data has become a critical global economic commodity; that 'cyber sovereignty' promoted by China, Russia and others threatens to disadvantage Japan in terms of access to global data flows; and that 'a Japan-alone approach [would] not be successful'.[103] China's growing weight in cross-border data flows adds to the importance of DFFT for Japan's economic security: at 23% of the global total, China's share is now nearly double that of the US.[104]

Japan's strategy seeks to build a critical mass of like-minded countries around DFFT that is large enough to outweigh China's inbuilt advantage from the volume of data generated by its 1.4bn-strong population and, ultimately, to force China to comply with DFFT rules in order to secure access to key markets. Because of their large populations, Japan must secure the support of the EU, the US and, ideally, India. Progress has, however, been slow. Although the Japan–EU Economic Partnership Agreement (EPA), launched in February 2019, was another landmark trade deal for Japan and contained digital economy provisions, differences over data privacy have hampered closer cooperation between the EU and the US. India, which remains sensitive regarding its own data sover-eignty and Western 'data colonialism', did not sign the 'Osaka

Declaration on the Digital Economy' along with Indonesia and South Africa, under which the signatories commit themselves to work towards improved global governance in digital commerce through the WTO.[105]

Japan's order-building is also visible in its loose association with Australia, India and the US in the Quad. The grouping has its roots in the humanitarian cooperation between the four countries in the wake of the 2004 Indian Ocean tsunami and was launched at Abe's initiative in May 2007 in Manila on the sidelines of the ARF with the aim of improving security coordination among the four partners. (The concept of the Quad aligns with historical strategic thinking by Alfred Thayer Mahan, who argued that cooperation between maritime democracies is important to balance against a continental hegemon.)[106] However, weak interest from Australia, India and the US, coupled with Abe's resignation as prime minister in September 2007, stalled further progress. Abe picked up the idea again in December 2012 immediately after his return to power when he outlined the concept of a regional 'Democratic Security Diamond', in which Japan 'as one of the oldest seafaring democracies in Asia' would join with Australia, India and the US to 'preserve the common good' in the Indian and Pacific oceans.[107] With emphasis on shared values and the strategic importance of the maritime space, the connection between the 'Democratic Security Diamond' and what later became FOIP is also apparent.

It was not, however, until 2017 that the Quad regained momentum among all its members, almost entirely as a result of growing shared concerns about China. This was evident in the increased frequency of high-level meetings and in the *Malabar* naval exercise in 2020, in which India invited Australia to participate for the first time alongside its usual partners, Japan and the US. Australia also participated in the 2021 *Malabar* exercise. US engagement with the Quad picked up after the installation of the Biden administration, with Washington then taking the initiative to convene the first Quad leaders' summit, which took place in virtual format in March 2021. This meeting was also notable for the broadening of the Quad's remit to include areas of economic security such as critical technologies, climate change and health.[108] This widening of the Quad's ambit, which in effect adds a geo-economic dimension to its geopolitical focus, will be important in terms of its potential role in balancing China's growing multi-dimensional power.

CHAPTER THREE

Japan's geo-economic strategy: implementation

Since 1945, successive Japanese administrations have adapted their geo-economic goals and means in accordance with the structural changes in Japan's geopolitical environment. However, for Japan's geo-economic strategy to be effective, implementation – the *ways* in which Tokyo uses its policy tools – also matters. In light of Japan's past experiences, recent changes in the geo-economic environment as a result of the 'fourth industrial revolution' (or the digital economy), the rapid economic, technological and military rise of China, and US–China strategic competition, have meant that four factors have exerted important influences over the degree to which the geo-economic strategy that took shape during Abe's second administration has been implemented effectively.

'Island nation' vs 'maritime power'

The first factor is the degree of 'outwardness' in Tokyo's foreign policy and thus Japan's ability to play the role of a regional and global geo-economic actor. A strong case may be made that an outward-looking foreign-policy posture is essential for an import-dependent island country like Japan. However, as

Kosaka Masataka wrote in his 1965 book *Kaiyō Kokka Nihon no Kōsō* ('Japan's Vision as a Maritime Power'), Japan has not always taken this course.[1] Kosaka compared two maritime countries on either side of the Eurasian continent, Japan and the UK, and argued that they had taken divergent historical paths in pursuing their foreign-policy interests, with Japan – as an 'island nation' (*shima guni*) – inclining in the Edo period (1603–1886) to a 'domestic-oriented foreign policy' (*naisei chūshin shugi*),[2] while Britain took a more outward policy (*soto no sekai de katsuyaku*) as a maritime nation (*kaiyō koku*) from the 1500s.[3] He warned against the former, arguing that 'two of the greatest tragedies in Japanese history, the isolation of Japan and the Manchurian Incident, both occurred when the outward-looking and inward-looking parts of Japan lost contact and balance'.[4] He further criticised the domestic- and economic-oriented foreign policy that had taken shape by the mid-1960s under the Yoshida Doctrine:

> Today, in the second half of the 20th century, Japanese politicians and its people are once again turning inward, and despite all appearances, Japan seems to be becoming more of an island nation. This may be the price of Japan's post-war efforts to focus solely on economic development while relying on the US for defence and diplomacy under its military power. Although Japan's post-war policies were extremely wise, they came at the cost of following the US and abandoning self-assertion.[5]

Japan's domestic-oriented posture during the 1990s, when policy energy was being increasingly absorbed by efforts to smooth the economic adjustment after the 1990 bubble collapse, and during the political instability that followed the Koizumi administration in the mid- to late 2000s, suggests that Kosaka's point is still valid in the twenty-first century. However, China's increasing assertiveness in Asia, coupled with the changing regional military balance in favour of Beijing, now means that an inward-looking Japanese government would present a significantly greater risk to regional and global stability than was the case in either the 1990s or the early 2000s. Unlike in the Cold War, the US does not enjoy the economic and military pre-eminence against China that it had against the Soviet Union and so must rely on allies and partners to help secure its interests in the region. China's rise has thus also increased Japan's regional strategic importance.

Furthermore, great-power competition in the twenty-first century differs from that of the Cold War in that China has become deeply embedded in the global economic system since its accession to the WTO in 2001. Although its economic maturation will bring with it slower GDP growth, China's economy also remains considerably more vigorous than that of the increasingly economically sclerotic Soviet Union in the 1970s or 1980s. While its defence budget is rising quickly and, at nearly US$200bn annually, is now the world's second largest, at just over 1% of GDP it remains small compared with the 10% or more of GNP that estimates suggest the Soviet Union was spending on defence in the 1980s.[6] In the Soviet Union, defence spending drained the civilian economy of resources; China, meanwhile, can afford to spend more. China is now seeking to use its growing power to change the global order in a way that is favourable to its interests. Moreover, inconsistent policies from the US in recent years have eroded US pre-eminence in the region, and the credibility of its claims to regional leadership.[7] Such a drastic change in the geopolitical environment created space for Japan, with Tokyo being perceived as a trusted strategic partner by many regional countries, to adopt an explicitly outward-looking posture during Abe's second administration that enabled it to play a more active geo-economic role as a regional and global stabiliser.[8]

Yet the rising importance of economic security in Tokyo's geo-economic strategy, driven by the intensification of US–China strategic competition since the early 2010s and by the global coronavirus pandemic since 2020, poses a challenge to its outward-looking approach.[9] Like the US and European countries, Tokyo is urging companies – albeit with only limited success so far – to repatriate the manufacturing of goods with national-security implications in order to boost economic security and resilience.[10] These goods include semiconductors and medical products such as personal protective equipment and pharmaceuticals. Strengthening defensive measures, such as export controls and foreign-investment controls, also risks closing the economy to outside sources of productivity-boosting innovation and know-how, both of which Japan needs in order to raise its weak long-term growth rate.[11] Tokyo's tightening of controls on exports of key materials critical for South Korea's electronics industry in 2019 is a case in point. Tokyo claims the move was made owing to concerns about these materials finding their way to North Korea, but to others the move looked like retaliation for a South Korean Supreme Court ruling that ordered Japanese firms to pay financial compensation to Korean slave labourers during the Japanese colonial period.[12]

Fragmentation vs integration

The second factor is the quality of coordination between Japan's key geo-economic actors – its government, businesses and academic institutions. Coordination has often been poor, which has created an impediment to the government's ability to take an integrated approach to policy formation. The stove-piped nature of Japan's ministries (collectively known as

Kasumigaseki) has long been a major obstacle for the government in dealing with geo-economic issues, which tend to fall under multiple ministries. For example, both MOFA and METI play important roles in advancing trade agreements and infrastructure financing. In terms of economic security, METI and the Ministry of Finance implement regulations relating to export control and foreign-investment screening, respectively. In the case of enhancing the security of critical infrastructure, the Ministry of Internal Affairs and Communications (MIC), the Ministry of Land, Infrastructure, Transport and Tourism (MLIT) and the Financial Services Agency (FSA) are all involved in their capacities as administrators of key infrastructural areas such as telecommunications, aviation and financial services. Of course, such fragmentation is not unique to Japan. But in Japan's case, it is aggravated by the country's post-Second World War pacifism and the resulting separation of the civilian- and economic-oriented ministries from their security and foreign-policy counterparts.[13]

From an institutional perspective, administrative reforms since the Hashimoto administration in the late 1990s were intended to increase governmental effectiveness by giving the prime minister greater authority to push through policy agendas over the heads of competing bureaucrats. Among the most important of these reforms was revising the Cabinet Law to give the prime minister the 'clear legal right' to initiate policies in the cabinet.[14] The creation of the Cabinet Office in 2001 to coordinate broad government policy and, at the same time, of the Council on Fiscal and Economic Policy (CFEP), which sits in the Cabinet Office and which the prime minister chairs, also strengthened the prime minister's control over economic policy formation. From a geo-economic standpoint, the establishment (again in 2001) of the Council for Science and Technology (CST) in the Cabinet Office, also chaired by the prime minister, was designed to help the government integrate its approach to science and technology R&D programmes across a wide range of applications, including elements of national security. The CST was reorganised in 2014, becoming the present CSTI.[15]

Japanese governments did not immediately make the best use of the mechanisms that these innovations provided. The 2001–06 Koizumi administration's policy focus was on the domestic economic agenda, such as privatisation of postal services and fiscal reform.[16] The 2009–12 DPJ government, which distanced itself from *Kasumigaseki*, lacked the necessary strong political base and stability to make the most of the new system. Abe's second administration was the first to make strategic use of the full range of these enhanced prime-ministerial powers, and the prime minister further bolstered executive control over policy through innovations such as the NSC in 2013 and the setting up of the TPP headquarters in the Cabinet Secretariat Office in 2015. These institutional reforms have been important in terms of allowing the government to integrate geo-economic strategy. Yet fragmentation remains. The absence of MOD from CSTI, for example, remains an obstacle to meeting the challenges posed by sensitive technology areas with military implications.[17]

Coordination between Japan's public and private sectors has also atrophied over the years. Close government–industry relations were an important tool for ensuring efficient allocation of resources during Japan's recovery from wartime devastation and then to sustain its high growth trajectory from the 1950s to the early 1970s. Political-economy scholars such as Ezra Vogel and Chalmers Johnson highlighted how the Ministry of International Trade and Industry (MITI) (renamed METI in the 2001 reorganisation of the ministries) played an essential role in crafting industrial policies in close cooperation with Japanese businesses.[18]

These efforts included identifying and choosing which industries to develop; providing government-backed financing; setting up 'deliberative councils' (*shingikai*) between government and industries; and sending retired officials to senior management positions, known as 'descent from heaven', or *amakudari*. MITI's industrial policy supported growth of the heavy and chemical industries and then supported Japan's shift to a knowledge-based economy in the high-growth period in the 1950s–1970s.[19] From the 1980s, MITI guided Japan's private sector to expand into other Asian markets by facilitating direct investment in Southeast Asia and the development of supply chains in the region. This activism was not purely driven by economic concerns, and it facilitated Japan's geo-economic goal to advance connectivity and economic growth in Southeast Asia as laid out in the 1977 Fukuda Doctrine.[20]

However, Japanese government–industry ties weakened from the 1980s. One reason for this was strong US government criticism of Japan's industrial policies, which it regarded as unfair and market-distorting.[21] US pressure led to Japan agreeing to Voluntary Export Restraint (VER) measures that limited Japanese exports of key products such as cars and semiconductors to the US. These spurred Japanese carmakers to boost production in the US and may have helped trigger the decline of the Japanese semiconductor industry – from a share of over 50% of global production in the 1980s, Japan's chip output had sunk to around 10% of the global total by 2021.[22] This in turn pointed to the limits of MITI's post-war industrial strategy of 'industrial adjustment' (*sangyō chōsei*) because the strategy implicitly needed the support of Japan's allies and partners.

Japanese administrative and financial-sector reforms in the 1990s also weakened the so-called 'iron triangle' (*seikangyō no tetsu no toraianguru*) relationship between politicians, bureaucrats and businesses. Although initiated partly in response to nudging from the US and the West, the reforms also reflected domestic pressure for change following a series of high-profile political-corruption scandals. Indeed, public ire at the LDP's failure to initiate reforms was one of the main reasons for its fall from power in 1993 for the first time since its formation in 1955. The erosion of the power of the LDP's factions from the late 1990s as a result of the 1994 lower-house electoral reforms reduced both the intensity of LDP–business interaction and the incentives for business to fund and lobby particular factions.[23] Policies to boost the role of the market in Japan's economy from the late 1990s, which included financial-sector reforms, and attempts to improve policy transparency also played a role in reducing government–business coordination. MITI's transformation to METI in the 2001 *Kasumigaseki* reforms, which signalled a reduction of the ministry's industrial-planning role, also served to weaken government–business links.[24]

The IT revolution in the 1990s was another important factor in this divergence between government and business. The emergence of the internet and information and communications technology (ICT) services was a catalyst for globalisation, allowing Japanese firms to boost their presence in global markets beyond Tokyo's reach. Another significant aspect was the diminished role of MITI in the IT revolution. Steven K. Vogel, a scholar of Japan's political economy, observes that the approach of MITI/METI to IT policy lacked coherence. This stymied bold reforms, which were in any case not favoured by Japanese domestic electronics giants, and contributed to the failure of Japanese industries to shift towards a business model better suited for the information age.[25] The fact that Japan currently trails its competitors in ICT services supports Vogel's charge that by 'abandoning its own state-led model and yet not adopting a liberal market model either, the government risked undermining Japan's comparative institutional advantages without cultivating a viable alternative'.[26]

Despite the importance of telecommunications as a category of critical infrastructure that matters for national security, Japan does not, for example, have a single telecommunications network supplier that can offer a full 5G package. Japan also relies on foreign servers for its data, such as Microsoft and Amazon from the US and even China's Tencent. Continued governance problems at Toshiba, a strategically important Japanese electronics firm with defence businesses and key technologies for future telecommunications such as quantum key distribution (QKD), are also a challenge.[27]

Businesses' frequent semi-illiteracy regarding geo-economics and security is a further weakness. In March 2021, it was revealed that Chinese contractors for the Japanese social-media service Line had been able to access user data from its servers since August 2018.[28] It is evident that loopholes remain in the latest regulations for foreign-investment screening. One example of this was the Japanese electronic-commerce company Rakuten's announcement of a capital injection from a subsidiary of the Chinese technology firm Tencent. The investment gave Tencent a 3.6% stake in Rakuten, which was above the 1% limit of the government's new notification guidelines.[29] This was possible because Tencent agreed not to participate in management decisions – the firm's investment was thus 'net investment' and so exempt from prior notification requirements. This case thus revealed the challenges for Tokyo in identifying deals involving security risks before agreements are made. Japan's NSS believes that Tencent could still have a say in the management of Rakuten's business.[30]

The divergence between government and business matters in a geo-economic context because, as one Japanese observer notes, 'in the geo-economics game, private companies are the main players'.[31] The weakening of government–industry ties also puts Japan at a strategic disadvantage with regard to China. Beijing's military–civil fusion strategy encourages its civilian firms to cooperate with state-linked defence industries, therefore optimising the deployment of resources and commercial technologies for military purposes. This strategy, together with China's high degree of integration into the global economy, allows Beijing to challenge the rules-based liberal international order from within.[32] This challenge partly takes the form of a push by Beijing to set rules in new areas where governance is still largely unformed and which have direct links to Japanese security and economic interests, such as digital and even green technologies.

Ideology

Institutional reforms can help resolve some of the challenges of policy effectiveness in Japan, but the fundamental challenge for Tokyo – the gulf between its civilian and defence sectors – remains. This gap reflects the deep and enduring domestic ideological divisions that appeared in Japan after the end of the Second World War. Thus, the third challenge is political – the tension between the persistence of anti-militarism on the one hand and the preference for Japan to become a 'normal nation' on the other.[33]

Japan's ideological tensions matter with regards to its geo-economic strategy because effective implementation of the strategy requires security underpinnings. One example is the security of the SLOCs that carry Japan's exports and imports and thus sustain its economy. Along with the cyber domain, SLOCs have been described as the soft underbelly of Japan's security policy.[34] The attacks against two oil tankers, one of which was Japanese owned, near the Strait of Hormuz in June 2019 during Abe's visit to the Iranian capital Tehran was a reminder of the security risks associated with Japan's long energy-supply chains.[35] China's recent aggressive pursuit of territorial claims and its militarisation activities in the East China and South China seas, through which much of Japan's trade flows, have also fuelled economic security concerns in Tokyo. Ideological divisions, coupled with post-war legal constraints, have, however, limited Japan's ability to defend its economic interests by ensuring the freedom of navigation in Japan's vital SLOCs, whether in the Gulf or the South China Sea. Strong anti-military sentiment remains in Japan – witness the protests outside the Diet during the debates on Abe's security reforms between 2013 and 2015.[36] The public was also divided on the dispatch of troops to the Gulf for intelligence-gathering activities following the oil-tanker attacks, with a small majority opposing action by Japan.[37]

Another example is the protection and development of Japan's competitiveness in technologies with potential for military purposes. Chinese policy in this area is explicit with its military–civil fusion strategy. The speed of China's technological advances and the US admission that it lags behind China in some technology areas make it all the more important for Japan, as the most important US ally in the region, to help enhance the overall deterrence posture of the US and its allies.[38] The long-running ideological clashes between the Japanese government on the one hand and the country's science community, which largely eschews research into technology with military applications, on the other places Japan at a strategic disadvantage with regard to China.

The declining participation of Japanese universities in the MOD-administered ATLA's National Security Technology Research Promotion Fund, a funding mechanism established in 2015 to facilitate basic research in advanced technology areas with potential for military use, is a prominent example of this structural block.[39] Even after ATLA expanded its funding capacity 18-fold, from ¥600m (US$5.3m) to ¥11bn (US$96.2m)

Figure 14: **National Security Technology Research Promotion Fund applications and funding size, by organisation, 2015–20**

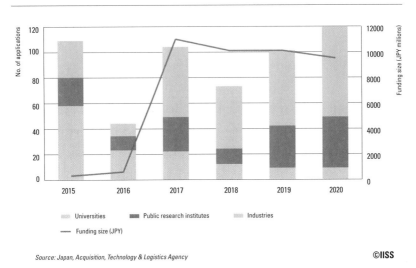

Source: Japan, Acquisition, Technology & Logistics Agency   ©IISS

in 2017, in order to foster basic research into dual-use technologies such as AI, sensors and quantum science, the number of participating academic institutions has continued to fall.[40] Japan's advanced technologies are developed in its civilian research institutes and commercial firms, and are largely kept separate from the defence industry.[41] Technology outflow from Japanese research institutions, which often lack expertise in understanding the potential dual-use applications of their research, is also of concern.[42]

Against this backdrop is the opposition of the Science Council of Japan (SCJ), the umbrella organisation for Japan's scientific community, to its members taking part in government programmes. In 2017, the SCJ released a document that repeated its 1950 and 1967 statements, which pledged that the SCJ 'will never become engaged in scientific research for military purposes' and highlighted its concerns around government intervention in ATLA's new research and development and funding mechanisms.[43] The 1950 statement followed the inaugural members' wish to 'contribute to peaceful recovery and the welfare of human beings' in the aftermath of the war. The 1960 statement was made to confirm the 1950 position after it was revealed that the 8th International Semiconductor Conference hosted in Kyoto by the Physics Society of Japan on behalf of the SCJ had received funding from the US armed forces to support US participants.[44] Reports that Japanese scientists have taken part in China's 'Thousands Talent Plan', which recruits international scientific expertise to undertake research in China, some of which will also have military applications, have predictably triggered allegations of double standards.[45]

Also important from a policy viewpoint is the disconnect between MOD and other security-related ministries in the making of the Japanese science and technology strategy. This is most glaring in CSTI, a ministerial-level body that manages a budget of ¥4trn (US$35bn) and drafts Japan's five-year Science and Technology Basic Plan for advancing national technology policy.[46] Japan Defense Agency directors-general – and, from 2006, the MOD's ministers – have been excluded from meetings of CSTI and its predecessor since the latter's establishment in 2001, even though prime ministers are given authority to invite any cabinet ministers to the council under Article 29 of the 1999 Cabinet Office Establishment Law.[47] The absence of the land, infrastructure and tourism minister and the health, labour and welfare ministers from CSTI's deliberations also looks like a strategic lacuna for Tokyo given the technological and security needs of both portfolios.[48]

Developments in space policy and capabilities, however, suggest that the bifurcation between civilian and defence agencies on dual-use technologies could narrow if the strategic environment surrounding Japan changes sufficiently. China's successful anti-satellite missile test against one of its own satellites in January 2007 was a strategic shock for Japan and highlighted the vulnerability of the extensive space assets of Japan and its ally, the US, both for defence and civilian purposes, such as communications, intelligence gathering, broadcasting, weather and disaster forecasts, and scientific research.[49] In response, Japan's Diet enacted the Basic Space Law in 2008 that highlighted the security aspect of space development[50] – a significant shift from the Diet's resolution in 1969 that pledged the non-military use of space.[51] Japan's 'National Defense Program Guidelines for FY 2019 and beyond' stated for the first time that the SDF should 'ensure superiority in use of space at all stages from peacetime to armed contingencies' and 'work to strengthen capabilities … to disrupt opponent's command, control, communications and information'.[52] Accordingly, MOD established the Space Operations Squadron under the ASDF in 2020 in order to enhance space situational awareness (SSA) and to coordinate space surveillance with US counterparts.[53] It also released plans to develop space-based early missile warning systems and space-based SSA.[54] These developments suggest that the critical nature of Japanese space assets for defence and commercial purposes contributed to Japanese society's and the science community's acceptance to use space for security purposes.

The US: enabler and constraint

While the foregoing factors derive from internal Japanese dynamics, the final element is external: the impact of the US on Japan's decision-making. Washington has tried both to encourage and to limit Japan's deployment of geo-economic power. In the case of the former, the US has helped Japan to improve its geo-economic literacy or to serve as a catalyst for Tokyo to take on important geo-economic issues. One example of the former is the importance of Japan joining the TPP/CPTPP for purposes of geo-economic competition with

China. Initially, when the LDP was in opposition from 2009–12, Abe was reluctant to join due to domestic opposition from agricultural interest groups, which long had close links with the party. However, Abe's appreciation of the TPP as a strategic framework to promote the rules-based economic order, coupled with his understanding of its potential role as a catalyst for economic reforms in Japan, persuaded him to change his position after his return to government in 2012, and Japan joined negotiations in 2013.

US intelligence capabilities have also helped Japan become more attentive to the potential military applications of advanced dual-use technology as well as to critical and emerging technologies developed in Japanese university laboratories that Japan ought to protect for strategic reasons.[55] US assertions on the strategic implications of the DSR, especially the spread of Chinese 5G, served to widen Tokyo's consideration of 5G from a relatively narrow focus on its implications for commercial telecommunications infrastructure to a broader perspective that appreciated its security implications for Japan's strategic infrastructure, according to a former senior Japanese government official.[56]

The US has also served as a spur for Japan to pursue more ambitious carbon-neutral goals to achieve the targets set by the 2015 Paris Agreement on climate change. The advent of the Biden administration and its prioritisation of climate-change policy was an important factor in persuading Tokyo to tweak its national energy strategy to achieve carbon neutrality by 2050.[57] To this end, in July 2021 Tokyo announced a programme for shifting the proportion of non-fossil fuels in Japan's energy mix to nearly 60% of the total by 2030, up from 44% in the previous plan and 24% in 2019.[58] The goals are ambitious, particularly given lingering public mistrust over nuclear power. But a firmer grip on climate-change policy in Tokyo will be important for

Japanese geo-economic strategy, particularly given the overlap between climate-change policy and technology policy, and the broader technological challenge from China.

However, the US has also sometimes constrained Japan's use of geo-economic power. Washington has, for example, periodically put pressure on Tokyo with the specific aim of restraining Japanese high-technology capabilities, owing to concerns that Japan is itself a geo-economic threat. Such fears were already evident in the 1960s and 1970s and acknowledged by the Japanese – in 1979, Okita Saburo, who was later foreign minister under prime minister Ohira, wrote of 'American anxiety about future competition from Japan in high-technology industries'.[59] Such pressure tends to rise when the US senses economic security challenges from Japan's growing dual-use technology capabilities. As well as US concerns over Japan's semiconductor industry in the 1980s, in the middle of that decade the US opposed Japan's proposal to develop the FS-X, an indigenous replacement for the ageing Mitsubishi F-1 fighter aircraft, out of fear that the growth of Japan's competitiveness in military technology could undermine US dominance in that sphere.[60] US concerns about Japanese technological advances were also partly driven by Tokyo's reluctance to transfer technology to the US due to its regulations on arms exports, which drove perceptions in Washington of a one-way high-technology transfer from the US to Japan.[61]

More recently, US sanctions against the new geo-economic great power, China, have also indirectly limited Japan's geo-economic strength. Examples of these sanctions include the Trump administration's unilateral sanctions against Chinese technology firms (such as the addition of Semiconductor Manufacturing International Corporation (SMIC) in December 2018 and Huawei in May 2019 to the Entity List) and its unilateral strengthening of its export control schemes.[62] Such actions have often been made without consulting the Japanese government and have directly impacted Japanese companies doing business in the US by disrupting supply chains. These decisions proved particularly challenging for Tokyo as the US also excluded Japan from its whitelist of countries that are exempt from tough investment screenings, even after the strengthening of Japan's export control mechanisms in 2019.[63]

CHAPTER FOUR

Japan's geo-economic effectiveness

Prime minister Abe Shinzo's second administration was one of the most transformative of Japan's post-Second World War governments in terms of foreign policy. As we have seen, geo-economic strategy was an important tool by which Abe sought to achieve his foreign-policy goals. Of these tools, the CPTPP mega trade deal may be the 'keystone', with de facto Japanese leadership of the bloc being a significant 'strategic asset' for the US in the region, according to veteran Japanese journalist Funabashi Yoichi.[1] Under Abe, Japan's pursuit of bilateral, regional and multilateral partners grew vigorously in both the economic and security realms. In addition to the CPTPP, the EPA with the EU and the Quad are good examples of this. 'Connectivity', one of the key pillars for FOIP, was a key ingredient in Abe's geo-economic strategy, both to support the international rules-based order and to increase Japanese agency within the bilateral security alliance with the US as a means of buttressing US presence in the Indo-Pacific. In enhancing connectivity, Abe was able to build upon Japan's good relations in the region – particularly Southeast Asia – that had been established as a result of the long record of Japanese ODA and private-sector investment flows. Abe's domestic institutional innovations, particularly the NSC and the NSS, also provided hitherto absent organisational support for this broadening of foreign policy.

This is not to say that Abe's geo-economic strategy was always successful. The cooling of relations with South Korea in 2019 over differences regarding the legacy of Japan's brutal occupation of Korea in 1910–45, for example, was a geo-economic setback for Tokyo. The proximate trigger for the deterioration was a disagreement in 2018 over the interpretation of the 1965 bilateral 'normalisation' treaty with regard to compensation claims arising from the occupation.[2] While differences over shared history between the two are not new, the quick spillover into bilateral economic and security relations was unprecedented: in addition to the placing of curbs on exports of key materials to South Korea already noted, Seoul announced in August 2019 it would cancel the bilateral General Security of Military Information (GSOMIA) intelligence-sharing agreement.[3] Subsequently, South Korea reduced its reliance on Japan for two of the three key materials in question by investing in domestic production facilities and import diversification.[4] The bilateral chill has done nothing to persuade Seoul to warm to Japan's Indo-Pacific concept and South Korea remains a noticeable absentee from the growing network of 'like-minded' Indo-Pacific countries broadly aligned with Japan. A more productive relationship with South Korea, with which it shares multiple interests, would buttress Japanese geo-economic influence in the region.

Abe's policy of rapprochement towards Russia was also unsuccessful. His courting of Russian President Vladimir Putin, which included economic inducements and no fewer than 27 Abe–Putin in-person meetings between 2006 and 2019, failed in its aim of finding a solution to the bilateral territorial dispute over the Northern Territories/Kurile Islands, which were annexed by Soviet forces at the end of the Second World

Figure 15: **Japan's demographic projections**

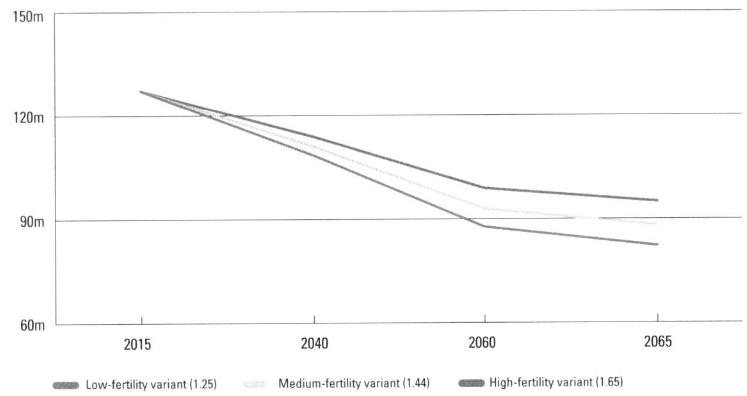

Low-fertility variant (1.25)   Medium-fertility variant (1.44)   High-fertility variant (1.65)

Source: Japan, National Institute of Population and Social Security Research   ©**IISS**

War. Changes to the Russian constitution, which took effect in July 2020 and prohibit the 'alienation of Russian territories', now preclude future Russian concessions on the issue. More than 70 years after the end of the Second World War, Russia and Japan thus have still not concluded a peace treaty. The failure to improve relations with Russia also leaves Japan's northern flank exposed, a strategic risk given Russia's increasing cooperation with China in military and other fields.

Abe's record in revitalising Japan's economy in order to boost national strength was also mixed. 'Abenomics' failed to boost productivity or to lift Japanese growth potential.[5] Indeed, in its April 2021 *Outlook for Economic Activity and Prices*, the BOJ estimated Japan's potential economic growth rate to be 'around zero percent or marginally positive'.[6] Abe's efforts to tackle demographic decline – one of Japan's most intractable structural challenges – were also half-hearted, despite his 2015 goal of stabilising Japan's population at around 100m by 2060.[7] Abe recognised the need to raise Japan's female labour force participation rate as a means of offsetting the overall decline in the country's labour force.[8] While there was a rise in the female labour force participation rate during Abe's second premiership, from 63.6% in 2012 to 72.8% in 2019, more than half of these jobs were in precarious part-time or temporary positions.[9] This, together with still-sparse and expensive childcare infrastructure, suggests little economic incentive for many to increase family size.[10] Meanwhile, although regulations were loosened under Abe's second premiership to allow more foreign workers into Japan, the numbers remain small in comparison to Japan's needs.[11] Japanese demographic decline thus looks set to continue, with even the government's National Institute of Population and Social Security Research forecasting a dip below 100m by 2053 and a further fall to 88m by 2065.[12] The headwinds to Japan's long-term growth prospects thus remain formidable.

Japan's external environment – flux and threat

Japan's external environment is highly dynamic, placing a premium on Tokyo's ability to adjust its geo-economic strategy so that it remains effective. This dynamism is fuelled particularly by China's drive to become the dominant power in Asia. President Xi Jinping's 'China Dream' of national rejuvenation, which he articulated in 2013 shortly after taking power, is premised on China 'catching up and overtaking' the West and thus prevailing in its great-power competition with the US.[13] This vision may not proselytise explicitly for regime change in the region to align governments more closely with Beijing, as was the case under Mao Zedong in the late 1940s and early 1950s.[14] But it does situate China as the potential regional hegemon, with the region functioning as a buffer to protect China against ideological, economic and military encroachment from the US. To this end, Xi has ramped up defence spending in support of China's ambitious programme of military modernisation, intended to make the PLA into a 'world-class' fighting force by 2049, the 100th anniversary of the founding of the People's Republic.[15]

China is also drawing the region more closely into its economic orbit. Trade links are already tight, with China being the largest export market or supplier of imports for many countries in the region. The RCEP mega trade deal agreed in November 2020 was a significant geopolitical as well as geo-economic win for China.[16] RCEP may have been initiated by ASEAN, but China's gravitational pull as the largest economy in the bloc will boost Beijing's role as a regional rule-setter. China's application to join the CPTPP in September 2021 is unlikely to succeed in the short term, as Japan and the other existing members will be reluctant to lower the hurdles for Beijing's accession by diluting the pact's high standards.[17] But China's move is consistent with its desire to exert hegemonic sway in the region. Beijing's Marxist political culture, in which relationships are viewed as 'competitive, necessitating struggle and dominance', adds a further layer of potency to the strategic challenge for the US-led and Japanese-supported liberal international order in the region.[18]

The keys to Japan's future geo-economic effectiveness

Aside from its own economic health, there are three main interlinked areas of focus when considering Japan's future geo-economic effectiveness. The first is Japan's security posture. Any change here is likely to remain incremental. Japan will continue to boost the capabilities needed to maximise Tokyo's contribution to the security alliance with the US and to balance the growing military threat from China. Ensuring Japanese technological inter-operability with the US, particularly in the domains of cyber and space, will remain a preoccupation for Tokyo. Christopher W. Hughes's observation from 2009 remains true: 'Japan is unlikely to diverge from or backtrack on its current trajectory of militarisation, channelled via the US–Japan alliance.'[19]

More fundamental change in Japan's defence posture might provide harder-edged support for future Japanese geo-economic strategy, but this would require a change to Article 9 of the constitution. Abe enjoyed overwhelming political dominance in 2012–20, which allowed him to fight and win six national elections during that period, but even he was unable to institute formal constitutional change despite the centrality of this to his desire of restoring the 'autonomy' that Japan lost after 1945.[20] This illustrated the considerable domestic political and procedural hurdles to constitutional change. Absent another prime minister with Abe's electoral clout, or perhaps a major external shock such as China using military force against Taiwan, formal change looks unlikely in the near term. That said, the constitution should not be seen as an insuperable obstacle to change in the future. Japanese governments have a long history of pragmatic constitutional reinterpretation when needed.

The second area of focus follows from the first and concerns Japan's unique difficulties with military–civil interaction. The challenge for Tokyo is made more acute by China's promotion of military–civil fusion as a channel for military development and to secure a broad competitive advantage against the US – witness China's 14th Five-Year Plan (2021–25), in which technology development and self-reliance, economic development and national security are all interlinked,[21] or its active recruitment of civilians to undertake scientific research for the military with the aim of driving innovation.[22]

The challenge for Japan is immense given the still-strong post-Second World War domestic ideological divisions that, for example, prevent its academic institutions from collaborating with the government on basic research with defence implications. Relatedly, post-1945 demilitarisation has left Japan with considerable legal and institutional constraints on its ability to develop 'offensive' capabilities, even in the cyber sphere.[23] The

Japanese government recognises the importance of being able to harness all-country expertise in boosting defence capabilities. The prominence given in the 2021 MOD white paper, *Defense of Japan*, to boosting research into 'advanced technologies' in areas such as AI, quantum science and cyber reflects this.[24] Such advanced technologies will not only be critical to economic health but will also be an arena for great-power competition over governance and influence. But the continued asymmetry in military–civil interaction between Japan and China disadvantages Japan and will constrain its geo-economic effectiveness.

The third focal area is Japanese industry, the resilience of which will be important for sustaining national geo-economic power. This has two main dimensions. The first is the relationship between Japan's government and the country's private-sector companies. Although coordination between the two was an important feature of Japan's developmental-state economic model in the initial post-war period, increasing investment by Japanese firms overseas and Japan's political and bureaucratic upheavals of the 1990s weakened government influence. This change was evident in the divergence between the interests of the Japanese government on the one hand and of business on the other in Tokyo's FTA policy of the early 2000s under the Koizumi administration. Initially, the FTAs prioritised countries that would produce only negligible gains for Japanese business and excluded the US and China, Japan's two largest markets. The muted response by mid-2021 to Tokyo's attempt to persuade Japanese firms to move production out of China to boost economic security, despite its siren call of financial inducements in 2020 to do so, is another example.[25] This divergence matters because of the ideological and commercial challenge of China's state capitalist economic model to the West, but also because of the increasing flow of advanced civilian technology into the military realm. There is therefore a need for a redefinition of the relationship between government and business in Japan that prioritises cooperation while avoiding the pitfalls of collusion and the erratic attempts of the former to 'pick winners'.

The second dimension is the resilience of Japan's industrial base in strategically important sectors. The automotive sector illustrates this well. Employing 5.4m people and accounting for around 8% of total employment in Japan, this is an economically vital sector as well as an important source of industrial innovation and export revenue.[26] Japanese automotive firms, having bet on hybrid technology as the successor to the combustion engine, are, however, lagging behind China in electric vehicles (EVs), a segment that Beijing has been aggressively supporting with a mixture of subsidies and mandates.[27] One observer cites the threat from EVs to Japan's automotive sector as a 'once in a lifetime challenge to Japan's industry and economy'.[28] That China is the main source of this challenge adds to the geo strategic risk for Japan of misreading the direction of the market.

The Japanese government is also trying to rebuild Japan's semiconductor sector, which has withered in recent years in the face of competition from Taiwan and South Korea, in order to bolster economic security. Its offer of a subsidy to Taiwan's TSMC, the world's largest semiconductor maker, of nearly ¥20bn (US$175m) to build an R&D facility in Tsukuba near Tokyo is a welcome recognition of the technology deficit that has been allowed to develop and of the economic vulnerability that this generates, particularly given China's efforts to boost its own advanced chip-making capabilities.[29] In October 2021, TSMC also indicated that it would build an advanced chip manufacturing plant in Japan in 2022, with operations due to start in 2024.[30] But moving Japan up the chip-making value chain and at scale will require a step change in the scale of financial support. TSMC's investment in Japan is, for example, likely to cost the firm around ¥1trn (US$9bn). The Japanese government talks of 'strategic indispensability' and 'strategic autonomy' as the twin pillars of the country's economic security, but neither is likely to be realised without closer government–business cooperation and significant injections of public funds to help companies foot the large costs and to bear the risks of developing advanced technologies.[31]

The increasing focus by the Japanese government on boosting economic security may drive fresh thinking in Tokyo on how best to resolve some of these issues. The installation of an economic security minister in Prime Minister Kishida's first cabinet in September 2021 reflected appreciation for the need to reinforce relevant policy coordination across government. The creation of such a portfolio was a global first and Japan's technology development is likely to be an early focus of the first minister in the role, Kobayashi Takayuki.[32] Maintaining economic and technological inter-operability with the US as a means of reinforcing the bilateral security alliance will presumably also inform the policy thinking of this new portfolio. Ensuring, however, that the focus on economic security does not become a proxy for autarky will also be important in promoting Japanese geo-economic effectiveness.

A template for middle powers

Finally, Japan's evolution as a geo-economic power offers lessons for middle powers. As the largest of the middle powers in terms of economic capability, Japan has played an important role in helping to sustain the multilateral order. Under Abe, Japan became an early mover in recognising that the strategic challenge from China lies in its geo-economic as well as its military power and in attempting to recalibrate Japanese tools of statecraft accordingly.[33] Abe's geo-economic insight echoes that of economist Albert O. Hirschman, who wrote in 1945:

'[t]here is no such thing as purely economic relations with the totalitarian states. Every business deal with them carries with it political, military, social, propaganda implications.'[34] This observation remains relevant for all powers seeking to calibrate their relations with China.

Japan's mobilisation of smaller countries to create coalitions of the 'like-minded' has worked as a force multiplier for its efforts to support the liberal international order, offering such countries an alternative to having to choose between supporting either China or the US. This strategy will become increasingly important as the twenty-first century progresses. The coming decades will bring unprecedented structural change to the global economy: by 2060, China, the US and India will be the largest economies – most probably in that order.[35] Each will be broadly as large or larger than the next five largest economies combined, creating fresh challenges for the next tier of countries as they seek to ensure continued global influence. Japan's ability to exercise geo-economic power effectively will therefore matter well beyond its immediate neighbourhood.

NOTES

Introduction

1. This forms the core of our definition of geo-economics. In our definition, geo-economics is different from mercantilism, in which economic advantage is the goal. See also Robert D. Blackwill and Jennifer M. Harris, *War by Other Means: Geoeconomics and Statecraft* (Cambridge, MA and London: Belknap Press of Harvard University Press, 2016), pp. 30–2, for a detailed discussion of why geo-economics is not 'some repurposed form of mercantilism'.

2. Cited in David A. Baldwin, *Economic Statecraft* (Princeton, NJ and Chichester: Princeton University Press, 1985), p. 51. In describing the evolution of the relationship between Japanese economic and foreign policy since the end of the Second World War, we will use the term geo-economics where applicable even where activity predates Edward N. Luttwak's coining of the term (see below).

3. Albert O. Hirschman, *National Power and the Structure of Foreign Trade* (Berkeley and Los Angeles: University of California Press, 1945/1980), p. 58. Despite its age, Hirschman's book repays study in light of his prescient comments on the difficulties of 'having purely economic relations with the totalitarian states' (p. 78).

4. Joseph S. Nye, 'Collective Economic Security', *International Affairs*, vol. 50, no. 4, October 1974, pp. 584–98, especially p. 588.

5. Paul Kennedy, *The Rise and Fall of the Great Powers: Economic Change and Military Conflict from 1500 to 2000* (New York: Random House, 1988), p. 439. Emphasis in original.

6. Edward N. Luttwak, 'From Geopolitics to Geo-economics: Logic of Conflict, Grammar of Commerce', *National Interest*, no. 20, Summer 1990, pp. 17–23.

7. Sanjaya Baru, 'Geo-economics and Strategy', *Survival: Global Politics and Strategy*, vol. 54, no. 3, June–July 2012, pp. 47–58.

8. The first oil shock of 1973, which was

triggered by the Organization of the Petroleum Exporting Countries' (OPEC) decision to impose an oil embargo on the US and other countries supporting Israel in the Yom Kippur War, threw this link into sharp relief. It was thus a major geo-economic turning point and forced Western governments to rethink policies around economic security. Writing in 1978, Japanese commentator Dr Funabashi Yoichi describes this new era as one of 'power economics' in which 'economic power is substituted for military power' [gunji pawā no 'daiyaku' toshite keizai pawā ga kakkō no dōgu toshite mukaeirerareyō toshite iru to miru beki na no ka]. See Funabashi Yoichi in his 1978 book *Keizai Anzenhoshō Ron – Chikyū Keizai Jidai no Pawā Ekonomikkusu* [Economic Security – the Era of Power Economics in the Global Economy] (Tokyo: Toyo Keizai Shinposha, 1978), pp. 292–5.

9   'Intimations of Mortality', *The Economist*, 30 June 2001, https://www.economist.com/special-report/2001/06/28/intimations-of-mortality.

10   'Prospectives', *Strategic Survey 2019: The Annual Assessment of Geopolitics* (Abingdon: Routledge for the IISS, 2019), pp. 11–18, especially p. 12.

11   McKinsey Global Institute, 'China and the World: Inside the Dynamics of a Changing Relationship', 1 July 2019, p. 9, https://www.mckinsey.com/~/media/mckinsey/mgi-china-and-the-world-full-report-feb-2020-en.pdf.

12   Joseph S. Nye, Jr, *The Future of Power* (New York: Public Affairs, 2011), p. 55.

13   Interview with Dr Funabashi Yoichi, Chairman, Asia Pacific Initiative, July 2021.

14   JTB Tourism Research & Consulting Co., 'Japan-bound Statistics', https://www.tourism.jp/en/tourism-database/stats/inbound/.

15   'Bei Chū 2 Kyō, Shikinryoku Tosshutsu, Nihon wa Gijitsu Kyōsō Taiba no Kiki' [US and China Leading in Spending Power, Danger of Japan Lagging Behind in Technological Competitiveness], *Nihon Keizai Shimbun*, 18 February 2020, https://www.nikkei.com/article/DGXMZO55791350Y0A210C2MM8000/.

16   Japan, Ministry of Defense, 'Defense of Japan (Digest)', p. i, 2021, https://www.mod.go.jp/en/publ/w_paper/wp2021/DOJ2021_Digest_EN.pdf.

17   Oriana Skylar Mastro, 'How China Is Bending the Rules in the South China Sea', *Interpreter*, The Lowy Institute, 17 February 2021, https://www.lowyinstitute.org/the-interpreter/how-china-bending-rules-south-china-sea. See also Japan, Ministry of Defense, 'Defense of Japan 2015', p. 119, https://warp.da.ndl.go.jp/info:ndljp/pid/11591426/www.mod.go.jp/e/publ/w_paper/pdf/2015/DOJ2015_1-2-3_web.pdf, for an example of the Japanese government's articulation of its concerns about China's land-reclamation work in the South China Sea.

18   Sarah Raine and Christian Le Mière, *Regional Disorder: The South China Sea Disputes*, Adelphi 436–7 (Abingdon: Routledge for the IISS, 2013), p. 58.

19   *Ibid.*, p. 12.

20   Eric Hobsbawm, *Age of Extremes: The Short Twentieth Century, 1914–1991* (London: Michael Joseph, 1994), p. 268; and Michio Royama, *The Asian Balance of Power: A Japanese View*, Adelphi Papers, no. 42 (London: International Institute for Strategic Studies, 1967), p. 2.

21   Kosaka Masataka, *A History of Postwar Japan* (Tokyo: Kodansha International, 1982), p. 223; and World Bank, 'GDP (Current US$) – Japan',

https://data.worldbank.org/indicator/
NY.GDP.MKTP.CD?contextual=simil
ar&locations=JP.

22 Christopher Wood, *The Bubble Economy:
The Japanese Economic Collapse* (Tokyo:
Charles E. Tuttle Company, 1993), p. 1.
At the bubble's peak the land occupied
in Tokyo by the Imperial Palace was
notionally worth more than the entire
state of California – see Bill Emmott,
*The Sun Also Sets: The Limits to Japan's
Economic Power* (New York, Toronto,
Sydney, Tokyo and Singapore: Simon
& Schuster, 1991), p. 118.

23 Organisation for Economic Co-oper-
ation and Development (OECD),
'Real GDP Long-term Forecast,
Total, Million US dollars, 2060 or
Latest Available', *Quarterly National
Accounts*, 2018, https://data.oecd.org/
gdp/gdp-long-term-forecast.htm.

24 The G7 includes Canada, France,
Germany, Italy, Japan, the UK and
the US. 'Japan Still World's Top
Creditor at End of 2019', *Japan Times*,
26 May 2020, https://www.japanti-
mes.co.jp/news/2020/05/26/business/
japan-worlds-top-creditor/.

25 See IMF, https://www.imf.org/exter-
nal/np/fin/quotas/2020/1027.htm;
World Bank Group, https://finances.
worldbank.org/Shareholder-Equity/
IDA-Voting-Power-of-Member-
Countries/v84d-dq44/data; and
United Nations Secretariat, https://
undocs.org/en/ST/ADM/SER.B/1023;
Asian Development Bank, https://
www.adb.org/documents/
adb-annual-report-2020.

26 OECD, 'Aid by DAC Members Increases
in 2019 with More Aid to the Poorest
Countries', 16 April 2020, https://www.
oecd.org/dac/financing-sustainable-
development/development-finance-
data/ODA-2019-detailed-summary.pdf.

27 Brad Glosserman, 'In the Competition
for Southeast Asia Influence, Japan Is
the Sleeper', *Japan Times*, 22 January
2020, https://www.japantimes.co.jp/
opinion/2020/01/22/commentary/
japan-commentary/competition-south-
east-asia-influence-japan-sleeper/.

28 'A Glimpse into Japan's Understated
Financial Heft in South-East Asia',
The Economist, 14 August 2021, https://
www.economist.com/finance-and-
economics/2021/08/14/a-glimpse-into-
japans-understated-financial-heft-in-
south-east-asia.

29 Mike Bird, 'Finance and Foreign
Policy Mix When China and Japan
Lock Horns', *Wall Street Journal*, 22
October 2020, https://www.wsj.com/
articles/finance-and-foreign-policy-
mix-when-china-and-japan-lock-
horns-11603356707?page=1.

30 Kosaka Masataka, *Options for Japan's
Foreign Policy, Adelphi Papers*, no. 97
(London: International Institute for
Strategic Studies, 1973), p. 7. It is
worth quoting the whole sentence as
Kosaka, writing in the early 1970s,
captures the oddness of Japan's position in international relations well:
'For one thing, it is difficult to understand a strange existence like Japan's
at all adequately. In psychological
terms it is probably not too difficult to
deal with a country which is powerful in a general sense, or even with one
which is weak in a general sense, but
Japan belongs to neither category.'

31 Japan, Cabinet Secretariat, 'The Constitution of Japan', 3 November 1946,
https://japan.kantei.go.jp/constitu-
tion_and_government_of_japan/
constitution_e.html.

32 'Other Basic Policies', Japanese Ministry of Defense, https://www.mod.go.jp/
en/d_policy/basis/others/index.html.

33 IISS, *The Military Balance 2021* (Abingdon: Routledge for the IISS), p. 23.

34 Tanaka Akihiko, *Japan in Asia: Post-Cold-War Diplomacy* (Tokyo: Japan Publishing Industry Foundation for Culture, 2017). Japan's SDF grew out of the National Police Reserve Force, which was formed in 1950 after US troops were moved out of Japan to fight in the Korean War. As Muraoka Kunio writes: 'Thus the initial step for the rearmament of Japan was made without the Japanese people realizing it.' The SDF was formed in 1954. See Muraoka Kunio, *Japanese Security and the United States, Adelphi Papers*, no. 95 (London: International Institute for Strategic Studies, 1973), p. 2.

35 Basic Law for the Federal Republic of Germany, https://www.gesetze-im-internet.de/englisch_gg/englisch_gg.html#p0723.

36 Germany, Bundesministerium der Justiz und für Verbraucherschutz [Federal Ministry of Justice and Consumer Protection], 'Gesetz über die parlamentarische Beteiligung bei der Entscheidung über den Einsatz bewaffneter Streitkräfte im Ausland (Parlamentsbeteiligungsgesetz)' [Act on Parliamentary Participation in Decisions on the Deployment of Armed Forces Abroad (Parliamentary Participation Act)], 18 March 2005, http://www.gesetze-im-internet.de/parlbg/BJNR077500005.html.

37 Bastian Giegerich and Maximilian Terhalle, *The Responsibility to Defend: Rethinking Germany's Strategic Culture*, *Adelphi* 477 (Abingdon: Routledge for the IISS, 2021), p. 43.

38 Japan, Ministry of Foreign Affairs, 'Japan–U.S. Security Treaty', 19 January 1960, https://www.mofa.go.jp/region/n-america/us/q&a/ref/1.html.

39 Victor D. Cha, *Powerplay: The Origins of the American Alliance System in Asia* (Princeton, NJ: Princeton University Press, 2016), p. 30.

40 Michael Leifer, *The ASEAN Regional Forum: Extending ASEAN's Model of Regional Security, Adelphi Papers*, no. 302 (Oxford: Oxford University Press for the IISS, 1996), p. 9.

41 See chapter one in Christopher W. Hughes, *Japan's Re-emergence as a 'Normal' Military Power, Adelphi* 368–369 (Abingdon: Routledge for the IISS, 2004), for a detailed discussion of the Yoshida Doctrine. Yoshida was also leader of the Liberal Party until its merger with the Japan Democratic Party in 1955 to form today's Liberal Democratic Party (LDP).

42 Hughes, *Japan's Re-emergence as a 'Normal' Military Power,* p. 22.

43 Yoshida referred to this domestic split as a '38th parallel', referencing the line of division between North and South Korea: 'Nihon wa kokudo koso futatsu no Nihon ni bunkatsu sarenakatta keredo, kokumin no naka ni futatsu no Nihon ga umare, kokumin no aida ni sanjūhachi dosen ga hikareteiru to itte yoi' [Although Japan has not been physically divided, two Japans have emerged within its people, and a 38th parallel has been drawn between them]. See Yoshida Shigeru, *Ōiso Zuisō: Sekai to Nihon* [Random Thoughts from Ōiso: The World and Japan] (Tokyo: Chūōkōron-Shinsha, 2015), p. 214.

44 Akihiko Tanaka, 'Rhetorics and Limitations of Japan's New Internationalism', *Japanese Studies Bulletin*, vol. 14, no. 1, 1994, pp. 3–33, especially p. 4.

45 Japan, Ministry of Foreign Affairs, 'Kokkai ni Okeru Naikakusōridaijin Oyobi Gaimudaijin no Enzetsu',

https://www.mofa.go.jp/mofaj/gaiko/bluebook/1987/s62-shiryou-101.htm; and Kenneth B. Pyle, 'In Pursuit of a Grand Design: Nakasone Betwixt the Past and the Future', *Journal of Japanese Studies*, vol. 13, no. 2, Summer 1987, pp. 243–70, especially p. 254.

46 Henry Scott Stokes, 'Japanese Decide to Permit Export of Military Technology to the US', *New York Times*, 15 January 1983, https://www.nytimes.com/1983/01/15/world/japanese-decide-to-permit-export-of-military-technology-to-the-us.html.

47 Clyde Haberman, 'Japan Set to Join "Star Wars" Plan', *New York Times*, 18 July 1986, https://www.nytimes.com/1986/07/18/world/japan-set-to-join-star-wars-plan.html.

48 See Mayumi Itoh, 'Japanese Constitutional Revision: A Neo-liberal Proposal for Article 9 in Comparative Perspective', *Asian Survey*, vol. 41, no. 2, March–April 2001, pp. 310–27, for a detailed comparative analysis of Nakasone's views on Japanese constitutional reform.

49 For example, Japan's acquiescence to the 1985 Plaza Accord, described in the Introduction, and the US–Japan semiconductor trade agreement of 1986, which is described in more detail in Chapter One. See also Michael J. Green, *By More than Providence: Grand Strategy and American Power in the Asia Pacific Since 1783* (New York: Columbia University Press, 2017), pp. 408–11.

50 Tanaka, *Japan in Asia: Post-Cold-War Diplomacy*.

51 This is well illustrated by the rise of the LDP's Seiwa Seisaku Kenkyūkai faction in the late 1990s. Between 2001 and 2020, the faction produced four of the LDP's six prime ministers in the period – Mori Yoshiro (2000–01), Koizumi Junichiro (2001–06), Abe Shinzo (2006–07 and 2012–20) and Fukuda Yasuo (2007–08). The faction traces its lineage back to the faction led by Abe Shinzo's grandfather, Kishi Nobusuke, who was LDP prime minister in 1957–60, and it was founded in 1962 by Fukuda Takeo (prime minister in 1976–78). See also Christopher W. Hughes, *Japan's Foreign and Security Policy Under the 'Abe Doctrine'* (Basingstoke: Palgrave Macmillan, 2015), pp. 9–11 for a detailed discussion of the rise of this faction.

52 Japan, Ministry of Defense, 'The Guidelines for Japan–U.S. Defense Cooperation', 23 September 1997, https://warp.da.ndl.go.jp/info:ndljp/pid/11591426/www.mod.go.jp/e/d_act/us/anpo/pdf/19970923.pdf. See https://warp.da.ndl.go.jp/info:ndljp/pid/11591426/www.mod.go.jp/e/d_act/us/anpo/pdf/19781127.pdf for the 27 November 1978 guidelines.

53 Hughes, *Japan's Re-emergence as a 'Normal' Military Power*, p. 9.

54 Japan, Ministry of Foreign Affairs, 'Campaign Against Terrorism: Japan's Measures', February 2002, https://www.mofa.go.jp/region/n-america/us/terro0109/policy/index.html.

55 Japan, Ministry of Foreign Affairs, 'The Issue of Iraq: Japan's Assistance Measures', December 2003, https://www.mofa.go.jp/region/middle_e/iraq/issue2003/assistance/2003.html.

56 Prime Minister of Japan and His Cabinet, 'National Defense Program Guideline, FY2005', 10 December 2004, https://japan.kantei.go.jp/policy/2004/1210taikou_e.html; Japan, Ministry of Defense, 'Chūki Bōeiryoku Seibi Keikaku (Heisei 17 Nendo–Heisei 21 Nendo) Ni Tsuite' [About the Mid-term Defence Plan,

FY2005–FY2009], 10 December 2004, https://warp.da.ndl.go.jp/info:ndljp/pid/11591426/www.mod.go.jp/j/approach/agenda/guideline/2005/chuuki.html.

57 'Explainer: Why Yasukuni Shrine Is a Controversial Symbol of Japan's War Legacy', Reuters, 15 August 2021, https://www.reuters.com/world/asia-pacific/why-yasukuni-shrine-is-controversial-symbol-japans-war-legacy-2021-08-13/.

58 The failure, owing partly to Chinese opposition, of Japan's efforts in 2005 to expand the 'ASEAN + 3' grouping (which involved China, Japan and South Korea as well as the ten ASEAN member states) to include Australia, India and New Zealand was a good example of this. Tanaka, *Japan in Asia: Post-Cold-War Diplomacy*. ASEAN's members are Brunei, Cambodia, Indonesia, Laos, Malaysia, Myanmar, the Philippines, Singapore, Thailand and Vietnam. Fraught relations between Japan on the one hand and China and South Korea on the other also hindered preparations for the first East Asian Summit (involving the leaders of the ASEAN states, Australia, China, India, Japan, New Zealand and South Korea) in 2005.

59 Prime Minister of Japan and His Cabinet, 'Policy Speech by Prime Minister Shinzo Abe to the 166th Session of the Diet', 26 January 2007, https://japan.kantei.go.jp/abespeech/2007/01/26speech_e.html.

60 Abe Shinzo, *Utsukushii Kuni E* [Towards a Beautiful Country] (Tokyo: Bunshun Shinsho, 2006), p. 28; and Japan, Ministry of Foreign Affairs, 'Japan Is Back: Policy Speech by Prime Minister Abe Shinzo at the Center for Strategic & International Studies (CSIS)', 22 February 2013, https://www.mofa.go.jp/announce/pm/abe/us_20130222en.html.

61 'Milestone Congress Points to New Era for China, the World', *China Daily*, 24 October 2017, https://www.chinadaily.com.cn/china/19thcpcnationalcongress/2017-10/24/content_33648051.htm; and Giulio Pugliese, 'Kantei Diplomacy? Japan's Hybrid Leadership in Foreign and Security Policy', *Pacific Review*, vol. 30, no. 2, March 2017, pp. 152–68, especially p. 160.

62 Royama, *The Asian Balance of Power: A Japanese View*, p. 6.

63 See Robert Hoppens, *The China Problem in Postwar Japan: Japanese National Identity and Sino-Japanese Relations* (London: Bloomsbury, 2015), pp. 5–7, for a discussion of how Chinese policy has had an impact on Japanese national identity.

64 H.R. McMaster, 'Japan: The Legacy of Japan's Longest Serving Prime Minister', Hoover Institution, 21 July 2021, https://www.hudson.org/research/17135-japan-the-legacy-of-japan-s-longest-serving-prime-minister. At around 9:25 minutes: 'When we look back at history we see many instances and cases where one side had a misunderstanding and underestimated the will and capability of the other side, and that eventually led to confrontation or disputes. So, in that context I do believe that it remains very important for us to make China realise Japan's determination and also have correct understanding about Japan's capability, and that will remain the key.'

65 Coral Bell, *The Asian Balance of Power: A Comparison with European Precedents*, *Adelphi Papers*, no. 44 (London: International Institute for Strategic Studies, 1968), pp. 2–3.

66 Abe, *Utsukushii Kuni E* [Towards a Beautiful Country], p. 29. 'Masa ni kempō no kaisei koso ga "dokuritsu no kaifuku" ga shōchō de ari' [Constitutional revision is a symbol of 'regaining independence']; see also pp. 123–44.

67 Japan, Ministry of Foreign Affairs, 'The 13th IISS Asian Security Summit – The Shangri-La Dialogue Keynote Address by Shinzo Abe, Prime Minister, Japan', 30 May 2014, https://www.mofa.go.jp/fp/nsp/page4e_000086.html.

68 Robert Ward, 'Japan's Security Policy and China', in *Asia-Pacific Regional Strategic Assessment 2021: Key Developments and Trends* (Abingdon: Routledge for the IISS, 2021), p. 39. The advantages conferred by Trump's abrasive policy towards China were evident in an anonymous piece written by 'Y.A.', a Japanese official, in *American Interest* in April 2020. As Y.A. notes: 'For countries on the receiving end of Chinese coercion, a tougher U.S. line on China is more important than any other aspect of US policy.' Y.A., 'The Virtues of a Confrontational China Policy', *American Interest*, 10 April 2020, https://www.the-american-interest.com/2020/04/10/the-virtues-of-a-confrontational-china-strategy/. Henry Kissinger's description of the role of a 'balancer' is also worth quoting in the context of the Japan–China–US triangle: 'a balancer cannot perform his function unless the differences among the other powers are greater than their collective differences with the balancer'. Henry Kissinger, *A World Restored* (London: Phoenix Press, 1957), p. 31. See also Singapore's founding father Lee Kuan Yew's 'isosceles triangle theory', which held that 'relations between Japan, the US and China are most stable when they take the form of an isosceles tri-angle. This means maintaining a triangular configuration in which US–Japan ties are closer than either Sino–Japanese relations or Sino–American relations.' Cited by Funabashi Yoichi in 'Foreign Policy Requires a Keen Sense of Balance', *Japan Times*, 10 February 2017, https://www.japantimes.co.jp/opinion/2017/02/10/commentary/japan-commentary/foreign-policy-requires-keen-sense-balance/.

69 See Abe, *Utsukushii Kuni E* [Towards a Beautiful Country], pp. 146–56 for discussion of his views on China. The quotation is from p. 151.

70 Japan, Ministry of Foreign Affairs, 'Regarding Discussions toward Improving Japan–China Relations', 7 November 2014, https://www.mofa.go.jp/a_o/c_m1/cn/page4e_000150.html; and Tsukasa Hadano, 'Xi Jinping Set to Make First State Visit to Japan in April', *Nikkei Asia*, 7 December 2019, https://asia.nikkei.com/Politics/International-relations/Xi-Jinping-set-to-make-first-state-visit-to-Japan-in-April.

71 Robert Ward, 'Abe Shinzo's Consequential Premiership', *9 Dash Line*, 10 September 2020, https://www.9dashline.com/article/abe-shinzos-consequential-premiership.

72 See 'Military–Civil Fusion Under Xi', *The Military Balance 2021* (Abingdon: Routledge for the IISS, 2021), pp. 19–21, for a detailed discussion of Chinese military–civil fusion policy. See also Meia Nouwens and Helen Legarda, 'Emerging Technology Dominance: What China's Pursuit of Advanced Dual-use Technologies Means for the Future of Europe's Economy and Defence Innovation', IISS–MERICS China Security Project, December 2018, https://merics.org/sites/default/files/2020-05/181218_Emerging_tech-

nology_dominance_MERICS_IISS.pdf.

73 Bell, *The Asian Balance of Power: A Comparison with European Precedents*, p. 12.

74 'Poll: China Viewed Unfavourably by Most in Japan', NHK World–Japan, 24 November 2020, https://www3.nhk.or.jp/nhkworld/en/news/backstories/1390/.

Chapter One

1 Christopher W. Hughes, *Japan's Remilitarisation, Adelphi* 403 (Abingdon: Routledge for the IISS, 2009), p. 22; and John Dower, *Embracing Defeat: Japan in the Aftermath of World War II* (London: Penguin Books, 1999), p. 77.

2 Victor D. Cha, *Powerplay: The Origins of the American Alliance System in Asia* (Princeton, NJ: Princeton University Press, 2016), pp. 142–8.

3 Kosaka Masataka, *Saishō Yoshida Shigeru* [Prime Minister Yoshida Shigeru] (Tokyo: Chūokōron-Shinsha, 2006), p. 71.

4 Osamu Nariai, *History of the Modern Japanese Economy* (Tokyo: Foreign Press Center Japan, 1994), p. 32.

5 See the following for the reference to the Economic Planning Agency's white paper: Jun Saito, 'Japan's Economy and Policy in a Global Context: Postwar Experience and Prospects for the 21st Century', Center for Strategic and International Studies, March 2017, https://csis-website-prod.s3.amazonaws.com/s3fs-public/160401_Japan_Economy_Policy_Global_Context.pdf.

6 *Ibid.*, p. 5.

7 Shinji Takagi, 'From Recipient to Donor: Japan's Official Aid Flows, 1945 to 1990 and Beyond', *Essays in International Finance*, no. 196, March 1995, Princeton University, p. 10, https://ies.princeton.edu/pdf/E196.pdf.

8 *Ibid.*, pp. 14–15.

9 Hiroyuki Hoshiro, 'The Ministerial Conference for the Economic Development of Southeast Asia and Japanese Diplomacy: Japan's Initiative and Its Limitations in the 1960s', *International Relations*, no. 144, February 2006, p. 11, https://www.jstage.jst.go.jp/article/kokusaiseiji1957/2006/144/2006_144_1/_article.

10 Royama, *The Asian Balance of Power: A Japanese View*, p. 5.

11 See, for example, Inoue Masaya, 'Kokuren Chūgoku Daihyō Mondai to Ikeda Gaikō – Kokufu "Bundan Koteika" Kosō o Megutte, 1957–1964' [The Chinese Representation Issue in the United Nations and the Ikeda Administration's Diplomacy, 1957–1964], *Kobe Law Journal*, vol. 57, no. 1, June 2007, p. 213, http://www.lib.kobe-u.ac.jp/infolib/meta_pub/G0000003kernel_81005064 .

12 So-called *LT bōeki* (LT Trade) required Japanese firms to accept China's three principles: 'The Japanese were not to (1) obstruct the establishment of diplomatic relations between Japan and the People's Republic of China; (2) participate in the formation of two Chinas; or (3) regard the People's Republic of China as an enemy'; quoted from Masaya Tsuchiya, 'Recent Developments in Sino-Japanese Trade', *Law and Contemporary Problems*, vol. 38, no. 2, Summer 1973, pp. 240–8, especially pp. 241–2, https://scholarship.law.duke.edu/lcp/vol38/iss2/6.

13 Glenn D. Hook et al., *Japan's International Relations: Politics, Economics and Security*, 2nd ed. (London: Routledge, 2005), p. 191; and Saito, 'Japan's Economy and Policy in a Global Context: Postwar Experience and Prospects for the 21st Century', p. 6.

14 See Jeffrey E. Garten, *Three Days at Camp David: How a Secret Meeting in 1971 Transformed the Global Economy* (New York: HarperCollins, 2021), pp. 26–44 for a detailed discussion on the United States' economic problems at the time.

15 *Ibid.*, p. 11.

16 Tanaka Akihiko, *Anzenhoshō: Sengo 50 Nen no Mosaku* [Security: Japan's 50 Years of Exploration in the Post-war Period] (Tokyo: Yomiuri Shimbunsha, 1997), pp. 269–71.

17 Saito, 'Japan's Economy and Policy in a Global Context: Postwar Experience and Prospects for the 21st Century', p. 7.

18 Funabashi, *Keizai Anzenhoshō Ron – Chikyū Keizai Jidai no Pawā Ekonomikkusu* [Economic Security – the Era of Power Economics in the Global Economy], pp. 292–5.

19 See National Graduate Institute for Policy Studies, 'The World and Japan' database, http://worldjpn.grips.ac.jp/documents/texts/docs/19770818.S1E.html for an English translation of Fukuda's 'Fukuda Doctrine' policy speech.

20 'Tai no ODA Donāka to Nihon no Shien ni Kansuru Kōsatsu' [An Analysis on Japanese Cooperation Towards Thailand as an Emerging Donor], *Fukuoka Daigaku Shōgaku Rongyō*, vol. 60, no. 3, March 2016, pp. 528–9, https://ci.nii.ac.jp/naid/120005739432.

21 Sueo Sudo, 'Japan–ASEAN Relations: New Dimensions in Japanese Foreign Policy', *Asian Survey*, vol. 28, no. 5, May 1988, pp. 509–25. See also 'The World and Japan' database for the report from Ohira's study group, https://worldjpn.grips.ac.jp/documents/texts/APEC/19800519.O1E.html.

22 Fukuda first stated this in his policy speech to the Diet in 1977; in his book *Atarashi Hoshu no Ronri* [Logic of the New Conservatives] (Tokyo: Kodansha, 1978), which was published before the LDP election in 1978, Nakasone writes: 'National security is based first of all on the consent and willingness of the people, and then on a comprehensive combination of diplomacy, economic cooperation, global public opinion influence operation, resource policy and other factors' (authors' translation). See Tanaka, *Anzenhoshō: Sengo 50 Nen no Mosaku* [Security: Japan's 50 Years of Exploration in the Post-war Period], p. 273.

23 *Ibid.,* pp. 276–7. Authors' translation.

24 *Ibid.*

25 *Ibid.*, p. 277.

26 Quoted in Tanaka, 'Rhetorics and Limitations of Japan's New Internationalism', p. 3.

27 Pyle, 'In Pursuit of a Grand Design: Nakasone Betwixt the Past and the Future', p. 244.

28 Bank of Japan, 'BOJ's Main Time-series Statistics', https://www.stat-search.boj.or.jp/ssi/mtshtml/fm08_m_1_en.html.

29 IMF, *Annual Report 1986*, p. 18, https://www.imf.org/external/pubs/ft/ar/archive/pdf/ar1986.pdf.

30 Interview with Dr Funabashi Yoichi, Chairman, Asia Pacific Initiative, July 2021.

31 Emmott, *The Sun Also Sets: The Limits to Japan's Economic Power*, p. 131.

32 'Japan Buys the Center of New York', *New York Times*, 3 November 1989, https://www.nytimes.com/1989/11/03/opinion/japan-buys-the-center-of-new-york.html.

33 Federal Reserve Bank of San Francisco, 'A Look at China's New Exchange Rate Regime', 9 September 2005, https://www.frbsf.org/economic-research/publications/economic-letter/2005/september/a-look-at-china-new-exchange-rate-regime/.

34 Murayama Yuzo, *Keizai Anzenhoshō o kangaeru: Kaiyōkokka Nihon no Sentaku* [Thinking about Economic Security: Japan's Choices as a Maritime Nation], (Tokyo: NHK, 2003), p. 59.

35 David E. Sanger, Clyde Haberman and Steve Lohr, 'A Bizarre Deal Diverts Vital Tools to the Russians', *New York Times*, 12 June 1987, https://www.nytimes.com/1987/06/12/world/a-bizarre-deal-diverts-vital-tools-to-russians.html.

36 'The Toshiba–Kongsberg Case', King's College London, 22 September 2014, https://www.kcl.ac.uk/news/the-toshiba-kongsberg-case; Murayama, *Thinking about Economic Security: Japan's Choices as a Maritime Nation*, p. 83; and Stuart Auerbach, 'Senate Approves 2-Year Ban on Toshiba's Sales in U.S.', *Washington Post*, 1 July 1987, https://www.washingtonpost.com/archive/politics/1987/07/01/senate-approves-2-year-ban-on-toshibas-sales-in-us/00e93986-4c8a-4365-99dd-4cdc5244fe4c/.

37 Douglas A. Irwin, 'The US–Japan Semiconductor Trade Conflict', National Bureau of Economic Research, January 1996, p. 5, https://www.nber.org/system/files/chapters/c8717/c8717.pdf. The Trump administration's imposition of targets for US–China trade under its Phase One trade deal with China in early 2020 had strong echoes of the United States' efforts to manage trade with Japan in 1986.

38 Murayama Yuzo, *Amerika no Keizai Anzenhoshō Senryaku – Gunji Henchō kara no Tenkan to Nichibei Masatsu* [US Economic Security Strategy: A Shift from a Military Focus and US–Japan Friction] (Tokyo: PHP Research Institute, 1996), p. 141.

39 *Ibid.*, p. 141.

40 The prime minister at the time, Kaifu Toshiki, took office following a series of scandals that had triggered the resignations of his two immediate predecessors, but was politically weak. The ruling LDP had also lost its majority in the upper house of the Diet, the House of Councillors, in 1989.

41 Yoichi Funabashi, 'Japan and the New World Order', *Foreign Affairs*, vol. 70, no. 5, Winter 1991/92, https://www.foreignaffairs.com/articles/asia/1991-12-01/japan-and-new-world-order.

42 Thomas L. Friedman, 'Baker Asks Japan to Broaden Role', *New York Times*, 12 November 1991, https://www.nytimes.com/1991/11/12/world/baker-asks-japan-to-broaden-role.html.

43 UN Security Council, 'Resolution 678 (1990) / Adopted by the Security Council at Its 2963rd Meeting, on 29 November 1990', https://digitallibrary.un.org/record/102245?ln=en.

44 See Samuel P. Huntington, 'Why International Primacy Matters', *International Security*, vol. 17, no. 4, Spring 1993, pp. 68–83, for a US critique of Japan's 'economic power maximization'. It is striking how similar Huntington's argument is to those now made about China's economic power.

45 APEC, the AMF and the CMI are all described in more detail in the next chapter.

46 See, for example, US president Bill Clinton's speech to the Paul H. Nitze

School of Advanced International Studies of the Johns Hopkins University on 9 March 2000 for an example of the optimism that economic integration into the world economy would also 'create positive change in China' in the United States' 'national interest': https://www.iatp.org/sites/default/files/Full_Text_of_Clintons_Speech_on_China_Trade_Bi.htm.

47 For views that considered the threat posed by the rise of China as being long term, see, for example, Shiraishi Takashi, *Umi no Teikoku: Ajia wo Dō Kangaeru ka* [Empire of the Seas: Thinking about Asia] (Tokyo: Chuko Shinsho, 2000), p. 195.

48 Japan's prominent post-war strategist Kosaka Masataka, for example, remained cautious about the rise of China in his 1969 essay *Kaiyōkokka Nihon no Kōsō* [Japan's Vision as a Maritime Country] and reiterated his concerns in the early 1990s. In his 1996 essay *Ajia Taiheiyō no Anzenhoshō* [Security in the Asia-Pacific], Kosaka stated that 'challenges from China will be the largest problem for Japan in the first half of the twenty-first century' ['Chūgoku mondai wa nijūisseiki zenhan no saidai no mondai']. See Iokibe Makoto and Nakanishi Hiroshi's edited volume, *Kōsaka Masataka to Sengō Nihon* [Kosaka Masataka and Post-war Japan] (Tokyo: Chūokōron-Shinsha, 2016), pp. 101–2 for reference to *Ajia Taiheiyō no Anzenhoshō*.

49 Seth Faison, 'China Sets Off Second Underground Nuclear Test in 3 Months', *New York Times*, 17 August 1995, https://www.nytimes.com/1995/08/17/world/china-sets-off-second-underground-nuclear-test-in-3-months.html; Barton Gellman, 'US and China Nearly Came to Blows in '96',

Washington Post, 21 June 1998, https://www.washingtonpost.com/archive/politics/1998/06/21/us-and-china-nearly-came-to-blows-in-96/926d105f-1fd8-404c-9995-90984f86a613/; Tsukasa Hadano, 'China Purges School Libraries of "Western Veneration"', *Nikkei Asia*, 18 April 2021, https://asia.nikkei.com/Politics/China-purges-school-libraries-of-Western-veneration2; and Kevin Sullivan, 'Japan's War Apology Disappoints Chinese', *Washington Post*, 27 November 1998, https://www.washingtonpost.com/archive/politics/1998/11/27/japans-war-apology-disappoints-chinese/f3b3eedc-de23-42b5-9100-b63d6eefcd67/.

50 Ward, 'Japan's Security Policy and China', p. 9.

51 Japan, Ministry of Foreign Affairs, 'Japan–China Joint Press Statement', 8 October 2006, https://www.mofa.go.jp/region/asia-paci/china/joint0610.html.

52 This phrase was used in the Japanese Ministry of Foreign Affairs' *Diplomatic Blue Book* until 2019; see, for example: p. 41, https://www.mofa.go.jp/mofaj/gaiko/bluebook/2019/pdf/pdfs/2_1.pdf.

53 Japan, Ministry of Foreign Affairs, '"Confluence of the Two Seas", Speech by H. E. Mr Shinzo Abe, Prime Minister of Japan at the Parliament of the Republic of India', 22 August 2007, https://www.mofa.go.jp/region/asia-paci/pmv0708/speech-2.html.

54 'The Japan–India Strategic Relationship with Dr Sanjaya Baru', *Japan Memo* podcast, IISS, 1 September 2021, https://www.iiss.org/blogs/podcast/2021/09/the-japan-india-strategic-relationship-with-dr-sanjaya-baru.

55 'India Top Recipient of Japanese Financial Aid Since 2003, Surpassing China', *Economic Times*, 26 March

2021, https://economictimes.india-times.com/news/india/india-top-recipient-of-japanese-financial-aid-since-2003-surpassing-china/article-show/81710675.cms?from=mdr.

56 Yukio Hatoyama, 'A New Path for Japan', *New York Times*, 26 August 2009, https://www.nytimes.com/2009/08/27/opinion/27iht-edha-toyama.html?pagewanted=1&_r=1.

57 Yoko Nishikawa, 'Q+A – What Is Japan's East Asia Community?' Reuters, 24 October 2009, https://www.reuters.com/article/us-asia-summit-japan-idUSTRE59N0IS20091024.

58 Justin McCurry, 'Japan PM Backtracks on Okinawa Military Base Pledge', *Guardian*, 4 May 2010, https://www.theguardian.com/world/2010/may/04/japan-okinawa-feud-us-base.

59 Keith Bradsher, 'Amid Tension, China Blocks Vital Exports to Japan', *New York Times*, 22 September 2010, https://www.nytimes.com/2010/09/23/business/global/23rare.html.

60 'Japan's Economic Statecraft', IISS *Strategic Comments*, vol. 26, no. 14, 10 July 2020, https://www.iiss.org/publications/strategic-comments/2020/japan-economic-statecraft.

61 Roel Landingin, 'Philippines vs China: Going Bananas', *Financial Times*, 11 May 2012, https://www.ft.com/content/7f801f57-b7fc-3a54-9634-56a15c41fd3e.

62 Shannon Tiezzi, 'It's Official: China, Not Japan, Is Building Indonesia's First High-speed Railway', *Diplomat*, 1 October 2015, https://thediplomat.com/2015/10/its-official-china-not-japan-is-building-indonesias-first-high-speed-railway/.

63 Kiran Stacey, 'China Signs 99-year Lease on Sri Lanka's Hambantota Port', *Financial Times*, 11 Decem-ber 2017, https://www.ft.com/content/e150ef0c-de37-11e7-a8a4-0a1e63a52f9c; 'Japan's Economic Statecraft'; for a Japanese perspective on the BRI's strategic implications, see, for example, Shino Watanabe, 'China's Infrastructure Development in the Indo-Pacific Region: Challenges and Opportunities', Center for Strategic & International Studies, March 2019, p. 7, https://csis-website-prod.s3.amazonaws.com/s3fs-public/FINAL_Working%20Paper_Shino%20Watanabe.pdf.

64 Japan, Ministry of Foreign Affairs, 'Extraordinary Press Conference by Foreign Minister Taro Kono', 14 April 2019, https://www.mofa.go.jp/press/kaiken/kaiken4e_000629.html.

65 Martin Fackler, 'Japan, Sticking with U.S., Says It Won't Join China-led Bank', *New York Times*, 31 March 2015, https://www.nytimes.com/2015/04/01/world/asia/japan-says-no-to-asian-infrastructure-investment-bank.html.

66 Hillary Clinton, 'America's Pacific Century', *Foreign Policy*, 11 October 2011, https://foreignpolicy.com/2011/10/11/americas-pacific-century/. 'The pivot to Asia' strategy was rebranded as 'the rebalance to Asia and the Pacific' in 2015: Office of the Press Secretary, 'Fact Sheet: Advancing the Rebalance to Asia and the Pacific', 16 November 2015, https://obamawhitehouse.archives.gov/the-press-office/2015/11/16/fact-sheet-advancing-rebalance-asia-and-pacific.

67 The White House, Office of the Press Secretary, 'Remarks by President Obama and President Xi Jinping of the People's Republic of China After Bilateral Meeting', 8 June 2013, https://obamawhitehouse.archives.gov/the-press-office/2013/06/08/remarks-presi-

dent-obama-and-president-xi-jinping-peoples-republic-china-. For concerns raised by Tokyo, see, for example, Brian Harding, 'The U.S.–Japan Alliance in an Age of Elevated U.S.–China Relations', Center for American Progress, 17 March 2017, https://www.americanprogress.org/issues/security/reports/2017/03/17/426709/u-s-japan-alliance-age-elevated-u-s-china-relations/.

68 John Ruwitch, 'China Bolsters East China Sea Claim, Warns of "Defensive Measures"', Reuters, 23 November 2013, https://www.reuters.com/article/uk-china-japan-idUKBRE-9AM02B20131123.

69 'Remarks As Prepared for Delivery by National Security Advisor Susan E. Rice: "America's Future in Asia"', The White House, President Barack Obama, 21 November 2013, https://obamawhitehouse.archives.gov/the-press-office/2013/11/21/remarks-prepared-delivery-national-security-advisor-susan-e-rice; and Hughes, *Japan's Foreign and Security Policy under the 'Abe Doctrine'*, p. 82.

70 See Introduction for details of Abe's security reforms.

71 Japan, Cabinet Secretariat, *Kisō Shiryō* [Basic Documents], October 2020, p. 12, https://www.kantei.go.jp/jp/singi/keizaisaisei/miraitoshikaigi/dai32/siryou1.pdf.

72 Rogier Creemers, Paul Triolo and Graham Webster, 'Translation: Cybersecurity Law of the People's Republic of China (Effective June 1, 2017)', New America, 29 June 2018, https://www.newamerica.org/cybersecurity-initiative/digichina/blog/translation-cybersecurity-law-peoples-republic-china/.

73 'National Intelligence Law of the P.R.C. (2017)', China Law Translate,

27 June 2017, https://www.chinalawtranslate.com/en/national-intelligence-law-of-the-p-r-c-2017/.

74 'Rūru Keisei Senryaku Giin Renmei to wa', *Nihon Keizai Shimbun*, 13 October 2020, https://www.nikkei.com/article/DGKKZO64917120S0A011C2PP8000/. See also Japanese Diet member Nakamura Hiroyuki's blog post for Amari's comments at the launch of the group: https://www.hiro-nakamura.jp/?tag=%E3%83%AB%E3%83%BC%E3%83%AB%E5%BD%A2%E6%88%90%E3%81%AE%E6%84%8F%E7%BE%A9. For Amari's views on China's digital development model and its export to Asia and beyond, see, for example, 'Dokusen Ichiman Ji: Keizaigaikō no Puro ga Kataru, Chūgoku Dejitaru Haken no Kyōi' [Exclusive: Economic Diplomacy Professional's View on Threat Posed by China's Digital Supremacy], *NewsPicks*, 13 August 2018, https://newspicks.com/news/3236775/body/.

75 US–China Economic and Security Review Commission (USCC), '2018 Report to Congress', November 2018, p. 266, https://www.uscc.gov/sites/default/files/annual_reports/2018%20Annual%20Report%20to%20Congress.pdf.

76 Arjun Kharpal, 'Power Is "Up for Grabs": Behind China's Plan to Shape the Future of Next-generation Tech', CNBC, 26 April 2020, https://www.cnbc.com/2020/04/27/china-standards-2035-explained.html.

77 USCC, 'PRC Representation in International Organizations', 20 April 2020, https://www.uscc.gov/sites/default/files/2020-04/PRC_Representation_in_International_Organizations_April2020.pdf.

78 Ministry of Foreign Affairs of the Peo-

ple's Republic of China, 'Global Initiative on Data Security', 8 September 2020, https://www.fmprc.gov.cn/mfa_eng/zxxx_662805/t1812951.shtml.

79 Funabashi Yoichi, 'China's Embrace of Digital Leninism', *Japan Times*, 9 January 2018, https://www.japantimes.co.jp/opinion/2018/01/09/commentary/world-commentary/chinas-embrace-digital-leninism/.

80 Danielle Cave, Fergus Ryan and Vicky Xiuzhong Xu, 'Mapping More of China's Tech Giants: AI and Surveillance', Australian Strategic Policy Institute, 28 November 2019, https://www.aspi.org.au/report/mapping-more-chinas-tech-giants; and Steven Feldstein, 'Testimony before the US–China Economic and Security Review Commission Hearing on China's Strategic Aims in Africa', USCC, 8 May 2020, https://www.uscc.gov/sites/default/files/Feldstein_Testimony.pdf.

81 Charlie Osborne, 'Japan Investigates Potential Leak of Prototype Missile Data in Mitsubishi Hack', *ZDNet*, 21 May 2020, https://www.zdnet.com/article/japan-investigates-potential-leak-of-prototype-missile-design-in-mitsubishi-hack/.

82 Yoshino Jiro, 'NEC, Mitsubishi mo Higai, Chūgoku Hakkā Shūdan no Zenyō' [The Full Story Behind China's Hacker Group Attacks on NEC and Mitsubishi], *Nikkei Business*, 7 February 2020, https://business.nikkei.com/atcl/gen/19/00002/020701079/.

83 Isabel Reynolds and Alyza Sebenius, 'Chinese Military Seen Behind Japan Cyberattacks', Bloomberg, 20 April 2021, https://www.bloomberg.com/news/articles/2021-04-20/chinese-military-seen-behind-japan-cyberattacks-nhk-says.

84 'Report on Research Funding Aims to Improve Transparency', *Japan News by the Yomiuri Shimbun*, 20 March 2021, https://the-japan-news.com/news/article/0007241292.

85 The idea that FOIP is a geo-economic concept will be discussed in detail in Chapter Three.

86 See, for example, The White House, 'National Security Strategy of the United States of America', December 2017, https://trumpwhitehouse.archives.gov/wp-content/uploads/2017/12/NSS-Final-12-18-2017-0905.pdf; and US Department of Defense, 'Summary of the 2018 National Defense Strategy of The United States of America: Sharpening the American Military's Competitive Edge', 2018, https://dod.defense.gov/Portals/1/Documents/pubs/2018-National-Defense-Strategy-Summary.pdf.

87 Japan, Ministry of Foreign Affairs, 'Japan Is Back'.

88 See 'Japan's Free and Open Indo-Pacific Vision at the Crossroads: Will It Endure After Abe?', *Strategic Survey 2020: The Annual Assessment of Geopolitics* (Abingdon: Routledge for the IISS, 2020), pp. 130–8; and 'Launch of *Strategic Survey 2020: The Annual Assessment of Geopolitics*', IISS, 20 November 2020, https://www.iiss.org/events/2020/11/strategic-survey-2020-launch.

89 This formulation is now frequently used by the Japanese government to articulate its concerns about China's activities.

90 Japan, Ministry of Foreign Affairs, 'Address by Prime Minister Shinzo Abe at the Opening Session of the Sixth Tokyo International Conference on African Development (TICAD VI)', 27 August 2016, https://www.mofa.go.jp/afr/af2/page4e_000496.html.

91 'The Japan–India Strategic Relationship with Dr Sanjaya Baru', *Japan Memo* podcast, IISS.

92 Takita Yoichi, 'Chūgoku no "Inryoku Ba" ga Nomikomu, Beikoku no Inūma ni Jinchi Kakudai' [China's Gravitational Pull Grows, China Expanding in the United States' Absence], *Nihon Keizai Shimbun*, 30 November 2020, https://www.nikkei.com/article/DGXMZO66744250X-21C20A1TCR000/.

93 Hugo Erken and Michael Every, 'Why India Is Wise Not to Join RCEP', RaboResearch – Economic Research, 29 December 2020, https://economics.rabobank.com/publications/2020/december/why-india-is-wise-not-to-join-rcep/.

94 Michael J. Green, 'Japan Is Back: Unbundling Abe's Grand Strategy', Lowy Institute for International Policy, December 2013, https://www.lowyinstitute.org/sites/default/files/green_japan_is_back_web_0_0.pdf.

95 Percentage calculated from the World Bank's database at https://data.worldbank.org/indicator/NY.GDP.MKTP.CD. Data is for 2019. See also James McBride, Andrew Chatzky and Anshu Siripurapu, 'What's Next for the Trans-Pacific Partnership (TPP)?', Council on Foreign Relations, 20 September 2021, https://www.cfr.org/backgrounder/what-trans-pacific-partnership-tpp.

96 Sebastian Strangio, 'At Annual Summit, US Stumbles on Engagement with Southeast Asia – Again', *Diplomat*, 16 November 2020, https://thediplomat.com/2020/11/at-annual-summit-us-stumbles-on-engagement-with-southeast-asia-again/.

97 President of the United States, 'National Security Strategy of the United States of America', December 2017, p. 46, https://trumpwhitehouse.archives.gov/wp-content/uploads/2017/12/NSS-Final-12-18-2017-0905.pdf;

US, Department of Defense, 'Summary of the 2018 National Defense Strategy of the United States of America', p. 9; see also US, Department of Defense, 'Indo-Pacific Strategy Report: Preparedness, Partnerships, and Promoting a Networked Region', 1 June 2019, https://media.defense.gov/2019/Jul/01/2002152311/-1/-1/1/DEPART-MENT-OF-DEFENSE-INDO-PACIFIC-STRATEGY-REPORT-2019.PDF.

98 Lindsey W. Ford, 'The Trump Administration and the "Free and Open Indo-Pacific"', Brookings Institute, May 2020, https://www.brookings.edu/research/the-trump-administration-and-the-free-and-open-indo-pacific/.

99 US Mission to ASEAN, 'Sec. Pompeo Remarks on "America's Indo-Pacific Economic Vision"', 30 July 2018, https://asean.usmission.gov/sec-pompeo-remarks-on-americas-indo-pacific-economic-vision/.

100 In January 2021, 66% of Chinese exports were subject to US tariffs and 58% of US exports were subject to Chinese tariffs. See Chad P. Brown, 'US–China Trade War Tariffs: An Up-to-Date Chart', 16 March 2021, https://www.piie.com/research/piie-charts/us-china-trade-war-tariffs-date-chart.

101 Japan, Ministry of Foreign Affairs, 'Treaty of Mutual Cooperation Between Japan and the United States of America', 19 January 1960, https://www.mofa.go.jp/region/n-america/us/q&a/ref/1.html.

102 US, Department of Commerce, Bureau of Industry and Security, 'Addition of Software Specially Designed to Automate the Analysis of Geospatial Imagery to the Export Control Classification Number 0Y521 Series', Federal Register, 6 January 2020,

https://www.federalregister.gov/documents/2020/01/06/2019-27649/addition-of-software-specially-designed-to-automate-the-analysis-of-geospatial-imagery-to-the-export.

103 *Ibid.*

104 Fifty-two Memorandums of Cooperation (MOCs) were signed between Japan and China for cooperation in third countries. See Japan, Ministry of Economy, Trade and Industry, '52 MOCs Signed in Line with Convening of First Japan–China Forum on Third Country Business Cooperation', 26 October 2018, https://www.meti.go.jp/english/press/2018/1026_003.html.

105 See, for example, Kawai Masahiro '"Ittai Ichirō Kōsō" to "Indo Taiheiyō Kōsō"' [One Belt One Road Vision and Indo-Pacific Vision], *World Economy Report*, vol. 2, Japan Institute of International Affairs, 8 May 2019, https://www.jiia.or.jp/column/column-348.html.

106 Steve Mollman, 'Japan's Buzzword of the Year Means "an Explosive Shopping Spree by the Chinese"', *Quartz*, 2 December 2015, https://qz.com/563304/japans-buzzword-of-the-year-means-an-explosive-shopping-spree-by-the-chinese/. Before the onset of the coronavirus pandemic in early 2020, inbound tourism had also been an important tool for revitalising Japan's economically struggling provinces. See, for example, 'Hōnichi Kyaku "Chihō e Chokkō" Kyūzō, 25% ga Shuyō 6 Kūkō Igai e' [Rapid Increase in Inbound Tourism Directly to the Regions, 25% Flying Directly to Airports Other than the Six Largest], *Nihon Keizai Shimbun*, 22 December 2019, http://www.nikkei.com/article/DGXMZO53565850Z11C19A-2SHA000/.

107 See, for example, Japan, Ministry of Foreign Affairs, *Diplomatic Blue Book*, 2019, p. 51, https://www.mofa.go.jp/files/000527147.pdf.

108 Funabashi Yoichi was one of the first to theorise 'economic security' in 1976. See Funabashi Yoichi, *Keizai Anzenhoshō Ron* [Theory of Economic Security] (Tokyo: Toyo Keizai Shinposha, 1978), pp. 292–301. Ohira's study group on comprehensive security also used the term economic security. See, for example, Tanaka, *Anzenhoshō: Sengo 50 Nen no Mosaku* [Security: Japan's 50 Years of Exploration in the Post War Period], pp. 276–7.

109 For a description of 'the Great Moderation', see 'Remarks by Governor Ben S. Bernanke', Federal Reserve Board, 20 February 2004, https://www.federalreserve.gov/boarddocs/speeches/2004/20040220/.

110 Interview with Terazawa Tatsuya, July 2021.

111 'Kitamura Shigeru (Zen Kokka Anzenhoshō Kyokuchō) "Keizai Anzenhoshō" to wa Nani ka?' [Kitamura Shigeru, Former National Security Advisor, on 'Economic Security'], *Bungei Shunju Digital*, 9 August 2021, https://bungeishunju.com/n/n8282e3583553.

112 See, for example, Kirk Lancaster, Michael Rubin and Mira Rapp-Hopper, 'Mapping China's Health Silk Road', Council on Foreign Relations, 10 April 2020, https://www.cfr.org/blog/mapping-chinas-health-silk-road.

113 See, for example, the mid-term report put together by METI: 'Sangyō Kozō Shingikai: Tsushō Boeki Bunkakai, Anzenhoshō Boeki Kanri Shōiinnkai Chūkan Hōkoku' [Industrial Structure Council, Commerce and Trade Sub-committee, Trade Security Management Sub-committee Mid-term Report], 10

June 2021, p. 3, https://www.meti.go.jp/shingikai/sankoshin/tsusho_boeki/anzen_hosho/pdf/20210610_1.pdf.

114 Murayama Yuzo et al., *Bei Chū no Keizai Anzenhoshō Senryaku* [US and China's Economic Security Strategy] (Tokyo: Fuyoshobo, 2021), pp. 207–29.

115 Authors' interview with Terazawa Tatsuya. See also Kitamura Shigeru's interview with *Bungei Shunju Digital*, 9 August 2021, https://bungeishunju.com/n/n8282e3583553; for white papers, see METI's 'White Paper on International Economy and Trade' for the years 2018, 2019, 2020 and 2021, which are available at https://www.meti.go.jp/english/report/index_whitepaper.html. For mentions of military–civil integration, see Japan, Ministry of Defense, 'National Defense Program Guidelines for FY 2019 and Beyond', p. 5, https://www.cas.go.jp/jp/siryou/pdf/2019boueikeikaku_e.pdf.

116 Cabinet Office, 'Integrated Innovation Strategy', 2018, p. 92, https://www8.cao.go.jp/cstp/english/doc/integrated_main.pdf.

117 Japan, Ministry of Economy, Trade and Industry, *Kizon Chitsujo no Henyō to Keizai Sangyō Seisaku no Hōkōsei* [Changes in the Existing Order and Direction of Economic and Industrial Policy], p. 10, https://www.meti.go.jp/shingikai/sankoshin/sokai/pdf/024_02_00.pdf; and Japan, Ministry of Economy, Trade and Industry, 'White Paper on International Economy and Trade 2019', November 2019, https://www.meti.go.jp/english/report/data/wp2019/wp2019.html.

118 Japan, Cabinet Secretariat, 'National Security Strategy', 17 December 2013, p. 20, https://www.cas.go.jp/jp/siryou/131217anzenhoshou/nss-e.pdf.

119 Japan, Ministry of Defense, 'Defense Technology Strategy: Towards Delivering Superior Defense Equipment and to Secure Technological Superiority', August 2016, https://www.mod.go.jp/atla/en/policy/pdf/defense_technology_strategy.pdf.

120 MOD's 'Defense of Japan, 2018' white paper flagged for the first time that 'rapid advancements in technological innovation are now spreading into military fields', and mentioned that China, Russia and the US are focusing on R&D in unmanned technologies, AI and stealth technologies 'that rely heavily on the development of civilian technologies': see Japan, MOD, 'Defense of Japan, 2018', p. 51, https://warp.da.ndl.go.jp/info:ndljp/pid/11591426/www.mod.go.jp/e/publ/w_paper/pdf/2018/DOJ2018_Full_1130.pdf. The paper also mentioned for the first time Chinese military–civil fusion, stating that the goal 'is said to have been upgraded to the national strategy': see MOD, 'Defense of Japan, 2018', p. 115. The National Defense Program Guidelines released at end-2018 stated for the first time that 'China is promoting civil–military integration policy in areas of national defense, science & technology and industry, and actively developing and acquiring cutting-edge technologies of potential military utility': see Japan, Cabinet Secretariat, 'National Defense Program Guidelines for FY 2019 and Beyond', p. 5. For MOD's efforts to enhance interactions between the civilian and military sectors, see, for example, Yuka Koshino, 'Is Japan Ready for Civil–Military "Integration"?', IISS Analysis, 3 August 2021, https://www.iiss.org/blogs/analysis/2021/08/japan-civil-military-integration.

Chapter Two

1   ASEAN was established in 1967 and its founding members were Indonesia, Malaysia, the Philippines, Singapore and Thailand.

2   ODA has played multiple roles for Japan, including as a means for recycling some of its current-account surpluses and hence to deflect political criticism of its trade policy, particularly from the US. Indeed, Japan's Ministry of Finance has even argued that these surpluses are necessary for Japan to keep funding global ODA and foreign direct investment needs. See Takashi Inoguchi, 'Japan's Role in International Affairs', *Survival: Global Politics and Strategy*, vol. 34, no. 2, Summer 1992, pp. 71–87, especially p. 74.

3   Takagi, 'From Recipient to Donor: Japan's Official Aid Flows, 1945–1990 and Beyond', p. 1; and OECD, 'Net ODA from DAC Countries from 1950 to 2020', https://www.oecd.org/dac/financing-sustainable-development/development-finance-data/Longterm-ODA.xls.

4   OECD, 'Development Co-operation Profiles: Japan', https://www.oecd-ilibrary.org/sites/b8cf3944-en/index.html?itemId=/content/component/b8cf3944-en.

5   See Hook et al., *Japan's International Relations: Politics, Economics and Security*, p. 231, for a discussion on Japan's 'tied' ODA.

6   Yukio Satoh, *The Evolution of Japanese Security Policy*, Adelphi Papers, no. 178 (London: International Institute for Strategic Studies, 1982), p. 30.

7   See Shigehisa Kasahara, 'The Flying Geese Paradigm: A Critical Study of Its Application to East Asian Regional Development', United Nations Conference on Trade and Development, no. 169, April 2004, https://unctad.org/system/files/official-document/osgdp20043_en.pdf, for a detailed discussion of Japan's 'flying geese' model.

8   Japan, Ministry of Foreign Affairs, 'Japan's Official Development Assistance: White Paper 2001', p. 105, https://www.mofa.go.jp/policy/oda/white/2001/contents.pdf; Japan, Ministry of Foreign Affairs, 'Reference Statistics' from 'Official Development Assistance (ODA): White Paper on Development Cooperation 2019', March 2020, pp. 8–12, https://www.mofa.go.jp/mofaj/gaiko/oda/files/100161439.pdf. Full white paper available at https://www.mofa.go.jp/policy/oda/page24_000074.html.

9   Kosaka, *Options for Japan's Foreign Policy*, p. 22.

10 Japanese investment into Southeast Asia had also been rising in the 1970s, largely displacing the US. In 1971, Japan held 15.4% of foreign investments in the region, compared with 36.4% for the US. By 1976, Japan's share had risen to 36.4%, while the United States' had fallen to 26%. See Walter LaFeber, *The Clash: US–Japanese Relations Throughout History* (New York: W. W. Norton & Company, 1997), p. 366.

11 The yen rose to a post-Second World War nominal high of ¥80:US$1 in early 1995. This rapid appreciation against the background of Japan's prolonged post-bubble-burst economic adjustment may have been one of the factors contributing to Japan's slip into prolonged deflation from the late 1990s.

12 Japan, Ministry of Foreign Affairs, 'Official Development Assistance (ODA), Economic Cooperation Program for China', October 2001, https://www.mofa.go.jp/policy/oda/region/e_asia/China-2.html.

13 Ezra F. Vogel, *Deng Xiaoping and the Transformation of China* (Cambridge, MA: Belknap Press of Harvard University Press, 2011), p. 309.

14 LaFeber, *The Clash: US–Japanese Relations Throughout History*, p. 377.

15 'Cable From Ambassador Katori to the Foreign Minister, "Prime Minister Visit to China (Conversation with Chairman Deng Xiaoping)"', 25 March 1984, Wilson Center, https://digitalarchive.wilsoncenter.org/document/118849.

16 See Eric Harwit, 'Japanese Investment in China: Strategies in the Electronics and Automobile Sectors', *Asian Survey*, vol. 36, no. 10, October 1996, pp. 978–94, for a discussion of Japanese investment in China in the 1980s and early 1990s.

17 Ward, 'Japan's Security Policy and China', p. 29. Literally translated, *seikei bunri* means 'the splitting of politics and economics'.

18 Royama, *The Asian Balance of Power: A Japanese View*, p. 6.

19 Vogel, *Deng Xiaoping and the Transformation of China*, pp. 297–310.

20 LaFeber, *The Clash: US–Japanese Relations Throughout History*, p. 377.

21 Shinichi Akiyama, 'Japan to End Official Development Aid to China', *Mainichi*, 23 October 2018, https://mainichi.jp/english/articles/20181023/p2a/00m/0na/016000c. See also 'Tai Chū ODA, 40 Nen de Maku, Taitō na Kankei de Tojō Koku Shien e' [The Curtain Falls on 40 Years of ODA to China, Now That China Is Developed, as Equal Partners China and Japan Will Work to Offer Aid to Developing Countries], *Nihon Keizai Shimbun*, 24 October 2018, https://www.nikkei.com/article/DGXMZO36829380T21C18A0PP8000/.

22 Richard Halloran, 'Tanaka's Explosive Trip', *New York Times*, 21 January 1974, https://www.nytimes.com/1974/01/21/archives/tanakas-explosive-trip-roots-of-the-antijapanese-outbursts-in.html.

23 These were the ASEAN–Japan Forum, the ASEAN–Japan Foreign Ministers Conference and the ASEAN–Japan Economic Ministers Conference.

24 Japan, Ministry of Foreign Affairs, '(5) Statement by Foreign Minister Taro Nakayama to the General Session of the ASEAN Post Ministerial Conference', 22 July 1991, https://www.mofa.go.jp/policy/other/bluebook/1991/1991-appendix-2.htm.

25 Leifer, *The ASEAN Regional Forum: Extending ASEAN's Model of Regional Security*, p. 53.

26 Japan, Ministry of Foreign Affairs, 'Diplomatic Bluebook 2001: Chapter 1. General Overview', https://www.mofa.go.jp/policy/other/bluebook/2001/chap1-c.html.

27 'Open regionalism' was first used in a speech by South Korea's president, Roh Tae-woo, on 11 November 1991 at the APEC Ministerial Meeting. See APEC, 'APEC Ministerial Meeting', https://www.apec.org/meeting-papers/annual-ministerial-meetings/1991/1991_amm.

28 Saori N. Katada, *Japan's New Regional Reality: Geoeconomic Strategy in the Asia-Pacific* (New York: Columbia University Press, 2020), p. 92, quoting Funabashi Yoichi.

29 Rush Doshi, *The Long Game: China's*

Grand Strategy to Displace American Order (New York: Oxford University Press, 2021), p. 102.

30   The World Bank's September 1993 report, 'The East Asian Miracle: Economic Growth and Public Policy', marked a high point of confidence in the region's growth model, which rested on 'the central role of government–private sector cooperation' and 'interventionist policies'. The full report is available at https://documents1.worldbank.org/curated/en/975081468244550798/pdf/multi-page.pdf.

31   The idea of an AMF was not new and had been floated along with the establishment of the ADB, and gained traction again in Japan in the 1980s: see Jennifer A. Amyx, 'Moving Beyond Bilateralism? Japan and the Asian Monetary Fund', *Pacific Economic Papers*, no. 331, September 2002, pp. 4–5, https://openresearch-repository.anu.edu.au/bitstream/1885/40431/3/pep-331.pdf. For a detailed discussion of Japan's 1997 AMF démarche, see Phillip Y. Lipscy, 'Japan's Asian Monetary Fund Proposal', *Stanford Journal of East Asian Affairs*, vol. 3, no. 1, Spring 2003, pp. 93–104, especially p. 98, http://www.lipscy.org/lipscy_amf.pdf. See also, for example, Japan's provision of economic aid to Hanoi under the auspices of the Fukuda Doctrine after the fall of Saigon in 1975. Washington, meanwhile, had imposed a trade embargo on Vietnam. Japan terminated the aid to Vietnam following its invasion of Cambodia in 1978.

32   Koichi Hamada, 'From the AMF to the Miyazawa Initiative: Observations on Japan's Currency Diplomacy', *Journal of East Asian Affairs*, vol. 13, no. 1, Spring/Summer 1999, pp. 33–50, especially pp. 33–4, https://www.jstor.org/stable/23257214?seq=1#metadata_info_tab_contents.

33   See China, Ministry of Foreign Affairs, 'Pro-active Policies by China in Response to Asian Financial Crisis', https://www.fmprc.gov.cn/mfa_eng/ziliao_665539/3602_665543/3604_665547/200011/t20001117_697864.html; and Kentaro Iwamoto, 'Looking Back at the "Asian IMF" Concept', *Nikkei Asia*, 22 June 2017, https://asia.nikkei.com/Economy/Looking-back-at-the-Asian-IMF-concept.

34   Philip Y. Lipscy, 'Reformist Status Quo Power: Japan's Approach to International Organizations', in Yoichi Funabashi and G. John Ikenberry (eds), *The Crisis of Liberal Internationalism: Japan and the World Order* (Washington DC: Brookings Institution Press, 2020), pp. 107–32, especially p. 115.

35   Eiichi Furukawa, 'How Mahathir Overcame the Asian Crisis', *Japan Times*, 18 July 1999, https://www.japantimes.co.jp/opinion/1999/07/18/commentary/world-commentary/how-mahathir-overcame-the-asian-crisis/.

36   Japan, Ministry of Finance, 'A New Initiative to Overcome the Asian Currency Crisis (New Miyazawa Initiative)', 3 October 1998, https://www.mof.go.jp/english/policy/international_policy/financial_cooperation_in_asia/new_miyazawa_initiative/e1e042.htm; and Hook et al., *Japan's International Relations: Politics, Economics and Security*, p. 242.

37   Shiraishi Takashi, 'The Asian Crisis Reconsidered', RIETI Discussion Paper Series 05-E-014, Research Institute of Economy, Trade and

Industry, April 2005, p. 11, https://www.rieti.go.jp/jp/publications/dp/05e014.pdf.

38 'The Joint Ministerial Statement of the ASEAN + 3 Finance Ministers Meeting', 6 May 2000, https://aseanplusthree.asean.org/wp-content/uploads/2020/01/The-Joint-Ministerial-Statement-of-the-ASEAN.pdf.

39 Chalongphob Sussangkarn, 'The Chiang Mai Initiative Multilateralization: Origin, Development and Outlook', *ADBI Working Paper Series*, no. 230, Asian Development Bank Institute, July 2010, p. 10, https://www.adb.org/sites/default/files/publication/156085/adbi-wp230.pdf; and Olivia Negus, 'The Chiang Mai Initiative Multilateralization (CMIM): If Not Now, then When?', Center For Strategic & International Studies, 1 September 2020, https://www.csis.org/blogs/new-perspectives-asia/chiang-mai-initiative-multilateralization-cmim-if-not-now-then-when.

40 Japan, Ministry of Finance, 'Internationalization of the Yen for the 21st Century', 20 April 1999, https://www.mof.go.jp/english/about_mof/councils/customs_foreign_exchange/e1b064a.htm.

41 *Ibid*.

42 Japan, Ministry of Finance, cited in Shinji Takagi, 'Internationalising the Yen, 1984–2003: Unfinished Agenda or Mission Impossible?', *BIS Papers*, no. 61, Bank for International Settlements, p. 75, https://www.bis.org/publ/bppdf/bispap61g.pdf.

43 Bank of Japan, 'BOJ's Main Time-series Statistics', https://www.stat-search.boj.or.jp/ssi/mtshtml/fm08_m_1_en.html.

44 Takagi, 'Internationalising the Yen, 1984–2003: Unfinished Agenda or Mission Impossible?', p. 83.

45 Zhang Xiaohui, 'Why RMB Internationalization Is Vital', *China Daily*, 21 May 2021, https://www.chinadailyhk.com/article/168807.

46 Yoichi Funabashi, 'Japan's Moment of Truth', *Survival: Global Politics and Strategy,* vol. 42, no. 4, Winter 2000–01, pp. 73–84, especially p. 77.

47 Akitoshi Miyashita, 'Gaiatsu and Japan's Foreign Aid: Rethinking the Reactive–Proactive Debate', *International Studies Quarterly*, vol. 43, no. 4, December 1999, pp. 695–732, especially pp. 718–25; and Kimie Hara and Geoffrey Jukes, 'New Initiatives for Solving the Northern Territories Issue between Japan and Russia: An Inspiration from the Åland Islands', *Pacific Forum Issues & Insights*, vol. 7, no. 4, April 2007, pp. 6–7, https://csis-website-prod.s3.amazonaws.com/s3fs-public/legacy_files/files/media/csis/pubs/issuesinsights_v07n04.pdf.

48 Christopher W. Hughes, Alessio Patalano and Robert Ward, 'Japan's Grand Strategy: The Abe Era and Its Aftermath', *Survival: Global Politics and Strategy*, vol. 63, no. 1, February–March 2021, pp. 125–60, especially p. 131.

49 The economic-reform emphasis early in Abe's second term also made political sense for him. An overfocus on security issues at the expense of the domestic economy was one reason for the collapse in support for Abe in his short-lived first administration in 2006–07.

50 Averages calculated by author from the Bank of Japan, 'BOJ's Main Time-series Statistics', https://www.stat-search.boj.or.jp/ssi/mtshtml/fm08_m_1_en.html.

51 Richard Sims, *Japanese Political History since the Meiji Renovation, 1868–2000* (London: Palgrave Macmillan, 2001), pp. 330, 355–6.

52 IMF, 'World Economic Outlook Database', April 2021, https://www.imf.org/en/Publications/WEO/weo-database/2021/April/select-country-group. Japan's overall fiscal position is more stable than the gross debt stock data suggests. Net debt is considerably lower, reflecting the government's large stock of assets, and most of the debt is held by domestic investors, now principally the BOJ.

53 See also OECD, 'Level of GDP per capita and Productivity', https://stats.oecd.org/Index.aspx?DataSetCode=PDB_LV, for cross-country comparisons of productivity with Japan.

54 United Nations, 'World Population Prospects 2019', 2019, https://population.un.org/wpp/Download/Standard/Population/.

55 David Atkinson, *Nihon Kigyō no Shōsan: Jinzai Kakuho x Seisansei x Kigyō Seichō* [Enabling Japanese Firms to Win: Securing of Employees x Productivity x Corporate Growth] (Tokyo: Toyo Keizai Shinposha, 2019). See also Bill Emmott, *Japan's Far More Female Future: Increasing Gender Equality and Reducing Workplace Insecurity Will Make Japan Stronger* (Oxford: Oxford University Press, 2020), pp. 11–30 for a detailed discussion of Japan's recent demographic trends.

56 'Did Abenomics Work?', *The Economist*, 5 September 2020, https://www.economist.com/finance-and-economics/2020/09/03/did-abenomics-work.

57 Atkinson, *Nihon Kigyō no Shōsan: Jinzai Kakuho x Seisansei x Kigyō Seichō* [Enabling Japanese Firms to Win:

Securing of Employees x Productivity x Corporate Growth].

58 Kanehara Nobukatsu, *Anzenhoshō Senryaku* [Security Strategy] (Tokyo: Nihon Keizai Shimbun Shuppan, 2021), p. 56.

59 See *ibid.*, p. 64 for a useful pictoral representation of the NSC's three-meeting hierarchy. For a breakdown of the frequency of the NSC's meetings by meeting type and subjects discussed since 2013, see Prime Minister of Japan and His Cabinet, 'Seisaku Kaigi', https://www.kantei.go.jp/jp/singi/anzenhosyoukaigi/kaisai.html. Unsurprisingly given the circumstances of the global coronavirus pandemic, of the 43 NSC meetings held in 2020, 19 were emergency-situation sessions. There were 18 Four-minister Meetings and six Nine-minister Meetings. In normal years, however, the Four-minister Meetings dominate in terms of frequency.

60 Mayumi Fukushima and Richard J. Samuels, 'Japan's National Security Council: Filling the Whole of Government?', *International Affairs*, vol. 94, no. 4, July 2018, p. 4, https://dspace.mit.edu/bitstream/handle/1721.1/119205/Japan%27s%20National%20Security%20Council%20REVISED%20%236%20for%20Jen%20Greenleaf%20DSPACE.pdf?sequence=1&isAllowed=y.

61 Richard J. Samuels, *Special Duty: A History of the Japanese Intelligence Community* (Ithaca, NY: Cornell University Press, 2019).

62 Kanehara, *Anzenhoshō Senryaku* [Security Strategy], p. 76.

63 The Act on the Protection of Specially Designated Secrets. See Samuels, *Special Duty: A History of the Japanese*

Intelligence Community; Hughes, Patalano and Ward, 'Japan's Grand Strategy: The Abe Era and Its Aftermath', p. 134.

64 Samuels, *Special Duty: A History of the Japanese Intelligence Community*, p. 133.

65 Ward, 'Japan's Security Policy and China', p. 35.

66 See Japan, Ministry of Foreign Affairs, 'The Guidelines for Japan–U.S. Defense Cooperation', 27 April 2015, https://www.mofa.go.jp/files/000078188.pdf; and Japan, Ministry of Defense, 'The Guidelines for Japan–U.S. Defense Cooperation', 23 September 1997.

67 Brad Glosserman, 'NSC Change Prepares Japan for New Global Realities', *Japan Times*, 1 April 2020, https://www.japantimes.co.jp/opinion/2020/04/01/commentary/japan-commentary/nsc-change-prepares-japan-new-global-realities/.

68 'Kokusai Kikan Jinji, Chūgoku Shudō wo Yokusei, Naikaku ga Senryaku Ritsuan' [Cabinet Formulates Strategy for Heading Off Chinese Leadership in International Institutions], *Nihon Keizai Shimbun*, 15 June 2020, https://www.nikkei.com/article/DGXMZO60345600V10C20A6SHA000/; and 'Kokusai Kikan no Nihonjin Ni Wari Zō, Chūgoku Ishiki, Kokuren Kikan Toppu wa Zero' [Japanese Staff at International Institutions Up 20%, with China in Mind, Japan Has No Representation at the Top of United Nations Agencies], *Nihon Keizai Shimbun*, 28 May 2021, https://www.nikkei.com/article/DGXZQOUA25DMT0V20C21A5000000/.

69 Japan, Ministry of Finance, 'Rules and Regulations of the Foreign Exchange and Foreign Trade Act', 24 April 2020, p. 12, https://www.mof.go.jp/english/policy/international_policy/fdi/kanrenshiryou01_20200424.pdf.

70 'Japan Restricts Land Deals Near Strategic Assets', *Nikkei Asia*, 16 June 2021, https://asia.nikkei.com/Politics/Japan-restricts-land-deals-near-strategic-assets.

71 'Japan to Restrict Use of Foreign Tech in Telecom, Power Grids', *Nikkei Asia*, 18 May 2021, https://asia.nikkei.com/Business/Technology/Japan-to-restrict-use-of-foreign-tech-in-telecom-power-grids.

72 'Japan to Limit Foreign Students' Access to Security-linked Tech', *Nikkei Asia*, 26 October 2021, https://asia.nikkei.com/Politics/Japan-to-limit-foreign-students-access-to-security-linked-tech.

73 'Chūgoku Haiteku de Sonzaikan, Shiea Shūi 12 Hinmoku, Nihon Nuku' [Chinese High-tech Makes Its Presence Felt, Has Leading Share in 12 Product Areas, Overtakes Japan], *Nihon Keizai Shimbun*, 12 August 2020, https://www.nikkei.com/article/DGXMZO62552800S0A810C2MM8000/.

74 Japan, Ministry of Economy, Trade and Industry, 'Cabinet Decision on the Bill for the Act on Promotion of Developing/Supplying and Introducing Systems Making Use of Specified Advanced Information Communication Technologies', 18 February 2020, https://www.meti.go.jp/english/press/2020/0218_001.html.

75 Government of Japan, 'Science, Technology, and Innovation Basic Plan', 26 March 2021, p. 52, https://www8.cao.go.jp/cstp/english/sti_basic_plan.pdf.

76 Koshino, 'Is Japan Ready for Civil–Military "Integration"?'.

77 'Japan to Set Up Advanced-tech Fund with Eye on Economic Security',

Nikkei Asia, 17 October 2021, https://asia.nikkei.com/Business/Technology/Japan-to-set-up-advanced-tech-fund-with-eye-on-economic-security.

78 Statement by Prime Minister Shinzo Abe to the North Atlantic Council, 'Japan and NATO: Toward Further Collaboration', 12 January 2007, https://www.nato.int/docu/speech/2007/s070112b.html.

79 Japan, Ministry of Foreign Affairs, 'Address by Prime Minister Shinzo Abe at the Opening Session of the Sixth Tokyo International Conference on African Development (TICAD VI)', 27 August 2016, https://www.mofa.go.jp/afr/af2/page4e_000496.html.

80 Japan, Ministry of Foreign Affairs, '"Confluence of the Two Seas", Speech by H.E. Mr Shinzo, Prime Minister of Japan at the Parliament of the Republic of India'.

81 Speech by Kanehara Nobukatsu, Assistant Chief Cabinet Secretary and Deputy Secretary-General of the National Security Secretariat, The Prime Minister's Office, to the Naval War College, US Navy, 'Towards the Free and Open Indo-Pacific', 26 November 2018. Quoted with the author's permission.

82 Japan, Ministry of Foreign Affairs, '"The Bounty of the Open Seas: Five New Principles for Japanese Diplomacy", Address by H.E. Mr Shinzo Abe, Prime Minister of Japan', 18 January 2013, https://www.mofa.go.jp/announce/pm/abe/abe_0118e.html.

83 For example, Kosaka Masataka, *Kaiyō Kokka Nihon no Kōsō* [Japan's Vision as Maritime Power] (Tokyo: Chūokōron-Shinsha, 2008), pp. 239–50; and Kosaka, 'Options for Japan's Foreign Policy', p. 2.

84 'Japan's Free and Open Indo-Pacific Vision at the Crossroads: Will It Endure After Abe?', *Strategic Survey 2020: The Annual Assessment of Geopolitics* (Abingdon: Routledge for the IISS, 2020), pp. 130–8, especially p. 131.

85 Japan, Ministry of Foreign Affairs, 'Free and Open Indo-Pacific', 1 April 2021, https://www.mofa.go.jp/policy/page25e_000278.html.

86 Japan, Ministry of Foreign Affairs, 'Japan's Security Policy', 6 April 2016, https://www.mofa.go.jp/fp/nsp/page1we_000079.html.

87 See Kanehara, *Anzenhoshō Senryaku* [Security Strategy], p. 258. See also John Lewis Gaddis, *George F. Kennan: An American Life* (New York: Penguin Press, 2012), pp. 258–62 for a discussion of Kennan's article.

88 See Japan, Ministry of Foreign Affairs, 'Address by Prime Minister Shinzo Abe at the Opening Session of the Sixth Tokyo International Conference on African Development (TICAD VI)'.

89 Japan, Ministry of Foreign Affairs, 'The 13th East Asia Summit', 15 November 2018, https://www.mofa.go.jp/a_o/rp/page4e_000945.html.

90 Japan, Ministry of Foreign Affairs, 'Extraordinary Press Conference by Foreign Minister Taro Kono', 14 April 2019, https://www.mofa.go.jp/press/kaiken/kaiken4e_000629.html.

91 'Japan Says Won't Decide on AIIB Until Corruption Addressed', Reuters, 7 June 2015, https://www.reuters.com/article/uk-g7-summit-japan-aibb/japan-says-wont-decide-on-aiib-until-corruption-addressed-idUKKBN0ON12P20150607.

92 Katada, *Japan's New Regional Reality: Geoeconomic Strategy in the Asia-Pacific*, p. 112.

93 Interview with Dr Funabashi Yoichi, Chairman, Asia Pacific Initiative, July 2021.

94 The name of the unit was changed in

July 2017 to *TPP Nado Sōgō Taisaku Honbu* after Japan and the EU had reached an agreement in principle on the Economic Partnership Agreement, which took effect in February 2019.

95 UK, Department of International Trade, 'Japan Will "Spare No Effort to Support the UK" in Joining the CPTPP', 31 July 2018, https://www.gov.uk/government/news/japan-will-spare-no-effort-to-support-the-uk-in-joining-the-cptpp.

96 'China Applies to Join Pacific Trade Pact to Boost Economic Clout', Reuters, 17 September 2021, https://www.reuters.com/world/china/china-officially-applies-join-cptpp-trade-pact-2021-09-16/.

97 Masaya Kato and Kosuke Takeuchi, 'With Eye on China, Japan Refuses to Ease TPP Rules for New Members', *Nikkei Asia,* 18 December 2020, https://asia.nikkei.com/Economy/Trade/With-eye-on-China-Japan-refuses-to-ease-TPP-rules-for-new-members.

98 The strategic importance of submarine cables is also evident in the one project so far financed under the Trilateral Partnership between Australia, Japan and the US: an undersea fibre-optic cable connecting the Pacific Island of Palau to the 15,000-kilometre-long Bifrost Cable, which will, when completed in 2024, run between Singapore and the US. Palau is important for US security because of its location in the 'second island chain' defence line; Japan, Ministry of Foreign Affairs, 'Speech by Prime Minister Abe at the World Economic Forum Annual Meeting: Toward a New Era of "Hope-Driven Economy"', 23 January 2019, https://www.mofa.go.jp/ecm/ec/page4e_000973.html; and interview with a senior Japanese government figure on 28 July 2021,

quoted on condition of anonymity.

99 Interview of a senior figure in the Japanese government, 28 July 2021. Quoted under condition of anonymity.

100 Japan, Ministry of Finance, 'G20 Principles for Quality Infrastructure Investment', https://www.mof.go.jp/english/policy/international_policy/convention/g20/annex6_1.pdf.

101 'Full Text: Keynote Speech by Chinese President Xi Jinping at APEC CEO Dialogues', *Xinhua,* 19 November 2020, http://www.xinhuanet.com/english/2020-11/19/c_139527192.htm.

102 EU, 'The Partnership on Sustainable Connectivity and Quality Infrastructure between the European Union and Japan', 27 September 2019, https://eeas.europa.eu/headquarters/headquarters-homepage/68018/partnership-sustainable-connectivity-and-quality-infrastructure-between-european-union-and_en; and US, Department of State, 'Blue Dot Network', https://www.state.gov/blue-dot-network/.

103 For a useful definition of China's 'cyber sovereignty', see Nigel Inkster, *The Great Decoupling: China, America and the Struggle for Technological Supremacy* (London: Hurst & Company, 2020), pp. 155–6.

104 Toru Tsunashima, 'China Rises as the World's Data Superpower as Internet Fractures', *Nikkei Asia,* 24 November 2020, https://asia.nikkei.com/Spotlight/Century-of-Data/China-rises-as-world-s-data-superpower-as-internet-fractures.

105 For a detailed discussion on India's aspirations for 'self-reliance in digital technologies', see Neha Mishra, 'India: Leading or Thwarting Data Governance and Digital Trade?',

Hinrich Foundation, 10 August 2021, https://www.hinrichfoundation.com/research/article/digital/india-leading-or-thwarting-data-governance-and-digital-trade/; see also WTO, 'Osaka Declaration on Digital Economy', June 2019, https://www.wto.org/english/news_e/news19_e/osaka_declration_on_digital_economy_e.pdf.

106 'Material Advantage: FOIP and U.S. Alliances in Asia', Center for Strategic & International Studies, 20 September 2021, https://www.csis.org/analysis/material-advantage-foip-and-us-alliances-asia.

107 Abe Shinzo, 'Asia's Democratic Security Diamond', Project Syndicate, 27 December 2012, https://www.project-syndicate.org/onpoint/a-strategic-alliance-for-japan-and-india-by-shinzo-abe.

108 US, White House, 'Quad Leaders' Joint Statement: "The Spirit of the Quad"', 12 March 2021, https://www.whitehouse.gov/briefing-room/statements-releases/2021/03/12/quad-leaders-joint-statement-the-spirit-of-the-quad/.

Chapter Three

1 Kosaka, *Kaiyō Kokka Nihon no Kōsō* [Japan's Vision as a Maritime Country] (Tokyo: Chūokōron-Shinsha, 2016).

2 *Ibid.*, p. 209.

3 *Ibid.*, p. 232.

4 *Ibid.*, authors' translation.

5 *Ibid.*, p. 233, authors' translation.

6 China's defence spending as a percentage of GDP is taken from *The Military Balance 2021* (Abingdon: Routledge for the IISS, 2021), p. 518. The estimate of Soviet defence spending relative to the size of its economy is taken from David Fewtrell, *The Soviet Economic Crisis: Prospects for the Military and the Consumer*, Adelphi Papers, no. 186 (London: International Institute for Strategic Studies, 1983), p. 9.

7 See, for example, Stella-maris Ewudolu, 'Survey: Asean Confidence in US Plummets Under Trump', *Asean News Today*, 12 May 2017, https://aseannewstoday.com/2017/survey-asean-confidence-in-us-plummets-under-trump/.

8 According to a survey poll taken in late 2020 and early 2021 by the ISEAS–Yusof Ishak Institute, Japan was the most trusted strategic partner 'in the hedging game against US–China rivalry' with 67% expressing 'confidence'. This compared with China, which had a 'confidence' score of just 17%. Sharon Seah et al., *The State of Southeast Asia: 2021* (Singapore: ISEAS–Yusof Ishak Institute, 2021), p. 5, https://www.iseas.edu.sg/wp-content/uploads/2021/01/The-State-of-SEA-2021-v2.pdf.

9 See, for example, Mireya Solís, 'China, Japan, and the Art of Economic Statecraft', Brookings Institute, February 2020, https://www.brookings.edu/wp-content/uploads/2020/02/FP_202002_china_japan_solis.pdf.

10 Ben Dooley and Makiko Inoue, 'Japan Is Paying Firms to Make Things at Home. But China's Pull Is Still Strong', *New York Times*, 26 September 2020, https://www.nytimes.com/2020/09/26/

business/japan-onshoring.html.

11 The decline in Japan's working-age population in 2018–50 is forecast by the Economist Intelligence Unit at around 1% per year. This, together with only modest productivity growth, points to a potential long-term GDP growth rate for Japan of under 1%.

12 'The Japan–South Korea Rift', IISS *Strategic Comments*, vol. 26, no. 1, January 2020, https://www.iiss.org/publications/strategic-comments/2020/japansouth-korea.

13 Kanehara, *Anzenhoshō Senryaku* [Security Strategy], p. 309.

14 Aurelia George Mulgan, *The Abe Administration and the Rise of the Prime Ministerial Executive* (Abingdon: Routledge, 2018), p. 11.

15 See Japan, Cabinet Office, 'Brochure about the Council for Science, Technology and Innovation', 2015, p. 1, https://www8.cao.go.jp/cstp/english/panhu/index.html, for details of CSTI's origins.

16 Takenaka Harukata, *Shushō Shihai Nihon Seiji no Henbō* [Prime Minister's Dominance: The Change in Japanese Politics] (Tokyo: Chuko Shinsha, 2006), pp. 58–60, 158–9.

17 As one observer caustically notes: 'CSTI doesn't do defence'. Interview with Kanehara Nobukatsu, July 2021.

18 See, for example, Ezra F. Vogel, *Japan as Number One: Lessons for America* (New York: Harper Colophon Books, 1979); Chalmers Johnson, *MITI and the Japanese Miracle: The Growth of Industrial Policy, 1925–1975* (Stanford, CA: Stanford University Press, 1982); and Daniel Okimoto, *Between MITI and the Market: Japanese Industrial Policy for High Technology* (Stanford, CA: Stanford University Press, 1989).

19 Johnson, *MITI and the Japanese Miracle: The Growth of Industrial Policy, 1925–1975*, pp. 311–15.

20 Shiraishi Takashi, *Umi no Teikoku – Ajia o Dō Kangaeurka* [Maritime Empire: How to Think about Asia] (Tokyo: Chuko Shinsho, 2000), pp. 135–6.

21 For US use of Section 301 against Japan, see, for example, Jean Heilman Grier, 'The Use of Section 301 to Open Japanese Markets to Foreign Firms', *North Carolina Journal of International Law and Commercial Regulation*, vol. 17, no. 1, Winter 1992, https://core.ac.uk/download/pdf/151515955.pdf.

22 Mitsuru Obe, 'Japan's Chip Industry Squeezed as Foreign Governments Boost Investment', *Nikkei Asia*, 10 September 2021, https://asia.nikkei.com/Business/Business-Spotlight/Japan-s-chip-industry-squeezed-as-foreign-governments-boost-investment.

23 See Bradley Richardson, *Japanese Democracy: Power, Coordination, and Performance* (New Haven, CT: Yale University Press, 1997), pp. 175–84, for a detailed discussion of the dynamics of Japan's business–LDP relations. See also pp. 15–16 of the same volume for details on the changes and why they were implemented.

24 Interview with Dr Funabashi Yoichi, Chairman, Asia Pacific Initiative, July 2021. See also 'Sōsai Sen ga Yurasu Habastu Seiji Tōwareru Seisaku no Kyūshinryoku' [LDP Presidential Election Rocks Faction Politics, Questions Over Whether Policies Could Serve as Unifying Forces], *Nihon Keizai Shimbun*, 9 September 2021, https://www.nikkei.com/article/DGXZQODE07CTU0X00C21A9000000/, for a discussion of how the electoral reforms of the 1990s reduced the income of the LDP factions, partly

reflecting declining contributions from business.

25 Steven K. Vogel, 'Japan's Information Technology Challenge', in Dan Breznitz and John Zysman (eds), *The Third Globalization: Can Wealthy Nations Stay Rich in the Twenty-first Century?* (New York: Oxford University Press, 2013), pp. 350–72.

26 *Ibid.*

27 Kaori Kaneko and Takashi Umekawa, 'Senior Japanese Lawmaker Accuses Toshiba Activists of Short-termism', Reuters, 24 June 2021, https://www.reuters.com/business/japan-senior-lawmaker-hits-out-toshiba-shareholders-calls-monitoring-activists-2021-06-24/.

28 'Line Silently Exposed Japan User Data to China Affiliate', *Nikkei Asia*, 17 March 2021, https://asia.nikkei.com/Business/Companies/Line-silently-exposed-Japan-user-data-to-China-affiliate.

29 See Chapter Two.

30 'Tencent Unit's Stake in Rakuten Sparks Fears Over National Security', *Asahi Shimbun*, 1 April 2021, https://www.asahi.com/ajw/articles/14322934.

31 Interview with Dr Funabashi Yoichi, Chairman, Asia Pacific Initiative, July 2021.

32 *Ibid.* See also Kanehara Nobukatsu, '"Anzenhoshō Sangyō Seisaku" no Ritsuan Isoge' [Urgent Need to Craft 'Industrial Policy for Security'], *Sankei Shimbun*, 30 June 2021, https://www.sankei.com/article/20210630-HAYYPSH3QRNAXLONOFMGIMXCKQ/.

33 Kenichiro Sasae, *Rethinking Japan–US Relations: An Analysis of the Relationship between Japan and the US and Implications for the Future of Their Security Alliance*, Adelphi Papers, no. 292 (London: Brassey's for the IISS, 1994),

pp. 58–9. From a domestic political perspective, the role of ideology in the making and the implementation of Japan's geo-economic strategy is not as consequential when compared with Japan's defence and security strategies. In the realm of security, the LDP's long-standing and dovish coalition partner, Komeito, served as a constraining factor for Abe's push to reform Article 9 of the Japanese constitution. Komeito did not, however, stand in the way of Abe's other security reforms. The party also supports the government's method of using 'economic diplomacy including economic security' (*keizai anzenhoshō o fukumu keizai gaikō nado no torikumi o susume*) to promote the rules-based economic order through FOIP and regional trade agreements. See also Adam P. Liff and Ko Maeda, 'Electoral Incentives, Policy Compromise, and Coalition Durability: Japan's LDP–Komeito Government in a Mixed Electoral System', *Japanese Journal of Political Science*, vol. 20, no. 1, March 2019, pp. 53–73, especially p. 56. Komeito entered into coalition with the LDP in 1999. The party has a close relationship with the Japanese lay-Buddhist organisation Soka Gakkai. See also Komeito, '2021 Lower House Election Manifesto', 2021, pp. 62–4, https://www.komei.or.jp/special/shuin49/wp-content/uploads/manifesto2021.pdf.

34 Kanehara, *Anzenhoshō Senryaku* [Security Strategy], p. 226.

35 John Bowden, 'Two Oil Tankers Reportedly Attacked Near Strait of Hormuz', *Hill*, 13 June 2019, https://thehill.com/policy/international/448313-two-oil-tankers-attacked-near-strait-of-hormuz.

36 For protests against the security bills, see, for example, Shunsuke Murai and Yuka Koshino, 'Thousands Gather Outside Diet in Heavy Rain for Last Chance to Protest Security Bills', *Japan Times*, 17 September 2015, https://www.japantimes.co.jp/news/2015/09/17/national/thousands-gather-outside-diet-heavy-rain-last-chance-protest-security-bills/.

37 'Jieitai Chōto Haken 57% Hantai, Kyōdō Seron Chōsa, Yūshi Rengō Kōsō Meguri' [57% Oppose Dispatching SDF to the Middle East, According to Kyodo's Poll Survey on Coalition of the Willing], *Tokyo Shimbun*, 19 August 2019, https://www.tokyo-np.co.jp/article/15252.

38 'American Hypersonic Weapons Development Continues to Lag with Serious Problems – Congressional Research Service Report', *Military Watch Magazine*, 18 July 2021, https://militarywatchmagazine.com/article/US-hypersonic-weapons-development-lags-CRS-report; and Katrina Manson, 'US Has Already Lost AI Fight to China, Says Ex-Pentagon Software Chief', *Financial Times*, 10 October 2021, https://www.ft.com/content/f939db9a-40af-4bd1-b67d-10492535f8e0.

39 Japan, Ministry of Defense, 'Research & Development', Acquisition, Technology & Logistics Agency, https://www.mod.go.jp/atla/en/policy/research_and_development.html.

40 Koshino, 'Is Japan Ready for Civil–Military "Integration"?'.

41 Companies within Japan's industrial conglomerates are essentially different firms with different CEOs. Thus, there are no spillover effects within the conglomerates.

42 'Report on Research Funding Aims to Improve Transparency', *Japan News*, 20 March 2021, https://the-japan-news.com/news/article/0007241292.

43 Science Council of Japan, 'Statement on Research for Military Security', 24 March 2017, https://www.scj.go.jp/ja/info/kohyo/pdf/kohyo-23-s243-en.pdf.

44 Konuma Michiji, 'Shoki jidai no Nihon Gakujutsu Kaigi to Gunji Kenkyū Mondai' [Early Days of the Science Council of Japan and Issues around Military Relevant Research], July 2017, p. 14, https://www.jstage.jst.go.jp/article/tits/22/7/22_7_10/_pdf/-char/ja.

45 'Kitamura Shigeru (Zen Kokka Anzenhoshō Kyokuchō) "Keizai Anzenhoshō" to wa Nani ka?' [Kitamura Shigeru, Former National Security Advisor, on 'Economic Security'], *Bungei Shunju Digital*, 9 August 2021, https://bungeishunju.com/n/n8282e3583553.

46 Kanehara, *Anzenhoshō Senryaku* [Security Strategy], p. 93.

47 Japan's Cabinet Office was established in 2001 as part of the broader reorganisation of government functions at the time. See Prime Minister of Japan and His Cabinet, 'Cabinet Office Establishment Law (Law No. 89 of 1999) (Excerpt)', 1999, https://japan.kantei.go.jp/policy/index/science/konkyo_e.html, for an English translation of the law.

48 See Japan, Cabinet Office, 'Members of the Council for Science, Technology and Innovation', https://www8.cao.go.jp/cstp/english/policy/members.html, for a full list of CSTI's members.

49 Mark Williams Pontin, 'China's Antisatellite Missile Test: Why?', *MIT Technology Review*, 8 March 2007, https://www.technologyreview.com/2007/03/08/226350/chinas-antisatellite-missile-test-why/.

50 See Government of Japan, 'Basic Space Law (Law No. 43 of 2008)', May 2008, https://stage.tksc.jaxa.jp/spacelaw/country/japan/27A-1.E.pdf for an English translation of the law.

51 See also Suzuki Kazuto, 'Uchū Kihonhō de Nihon no Uchū Kaihatsu wa Kawaru ka' [Will the Basic Space Law Change Japan's Space Development?], Science Portal, 21 May 2008, https://scienceportal.jst.go.jp/explore/opinion/20080521_02/.

52 Japan, Cabinet Secretariat, 'National Defense Program Guidelines for FY 2019 and Beyond', p. 20.

53 Eric Johnston, 'Japan's New Space Squadron Takes a Giant Leap Forward', Japan Times, 2 June 2020, https://www.japantimes.co.jp/news/2020/06/02/national/japan-space-force-self-defense-forces/.

54 From a purely technological perspective, the US-based Center for Strategic & International Studies (CSIS)'s annual space threat assessment pointed out in 2019 that the Japan Aerospace Exploration Agency (JAXA)'s space capabilities could be applied to counter-space weapons systems. This includes a capability developed in 1998 that could 'rendezvous and successfully dock two orbiting satellites' or 'a robotic arm that could grapple and exercise coordinated control over a second satellite', although Japan has neither the plan nor the policy to use them for military purposes. See, for example, Todd Harrison et al., 'Space Threat Assessment 2019', Center for Strategic & International Studies, April 2019, p. 38, https://csis-website-prod.s3.amazonaws.com/s3fs-public/publication/190404_SpaceThreatAssessment_interior.pdf.

55 Kanehara Nobukatsu, 'Kagaku Gijutsu to Anzenhoshō, Minsei Gijutsu no Kanri/Ikusei ga Kyūmu' [Civilian Technology Management and Development Is an Urgent Task for Science and Technology Security], Nikkei, 10 April 2020, https://www.nikkei.com/article/DGXKZO57867440Z00C20A4KE8000/.

56 Interview with Terazawa Tatsuya, July 2021.

57 Maeda Yudai, 'Onshitsu Kōka Gasu Sakugen "46%" Mokuhyō no Shōgeki, Naze Nihon wa Noriokureta no ka' [The Shock of '46%' Reduction Goal of Carbon Emission. Why Did Japan Fall Behind?], Chuo Koron, 14 July 2021, https://chuokoron.jp/politics/117748.html.

58 '"Datsutanso Dengen 6 Wari" Takai Hādoru, Onshitsu Gasu Mokuhyō ga Senkō, Gyakusan de Sakutei' [60% of Electricity to Be Generated by Non-fossil Fuel, a High Hurdle, Meeting the Goals for Greenhouse Gas Emission Takes Priority, (the Basic Energy Plan) Crafted through Calculating Back from the Final Goal], Asahi Shimbun, 22 July 2021, https://www.asahi.com/sp/articles/DA3S14983936.html.

59 Saburo Okita, 'Japan, China and the United States: Economic Relations and Prospects', Foreign Affairs, vol. 57, no. 5, Summer 1979, https://www.foreignaffairs.com/articles/china/1979-06-01/japan-china-and-united-states-economic-relations-and-prospects.

60 See, for example, Mark A. Lorell, Troubled Partnership: A History of U.S.–Japan Collaboration on the FS-X Fighter (Santa Monica, CA: RAND, 1995), pp. 97–128.

61 Ibid., pp. 9–48.

62 Businesses, research institutions, private organisations, individuals

and other persons listed in the Entity List are subject to licencing requirements for the export, re-export and transfer of specific items. See, for example, US, Bureau of Industry and Security, 'Entity List', https://www.bis.doc.gov/index.php/policy-guidance/lists-of-parties-of-concern/entity-list for descriptions of the Entity List; see also US, Bureau of Industry and Security, 'Huawei Entity List Frequently Asked Questions (FAQs)', 3 December 2020, https://www.bis.doc.gov/index.php/documents/pdfs/2447-huawei-entity-listing-faqs/file; and US, Department of Commerce, 'Commerce Adds China's SMIC to the Entity List, Restricting Access to Key Enabling U.S. Technology', 18 December 2020, https://2017-2021.commerce.gov/news/press-releases/2020/12/commerce-adds-chinas-smic-entity-list-restricting-access-key-enabling.html.

63 Natsuko Segawa, 'Japan Excluded from New US Foreign Investment Whitelist', *Nikkei Asia*, 25 January 2020, https://asia.nikkei.com/Politics/International-relations/Japan-excluded-from-new-US-foreign-investment-whitelist.

Chapter Four

1 Interview with Dr Funabashi Yoichi, Chairman, Asia Pacific Initiative, July 2021; Hughes, Patalano and Ward, 'Japan's Grand Strategy: The Abe Era and Its Aftermath', p. 135.

2 See 'The Japan–South Korea Rift', https://www.iiss.org/publications/strategic-comments/2020/japansouthkorea, for a detailed discussion on the background to the 2018–19 deterioration in bilateral relations.

3 The Japan–South Korea GSOMIA sets out a legal basis for intelligence sharing and is seen as an important strategic support to US defence capacity in the region.

4 Kim Young-bae, 'S. Korea's Materials and Components Reliance on Japan Declined Across the Board Since 2019 Trade Dispute', *Hankyoreh*, 28 June 2021, https://english.hani.co.kr/arti/english_edition/e_business/1001222.html.

5 'Did Abenomics work?', *The Economist*, 5 September 2020, https://www.economist.com/finance-and-economics/2020/09/03/did-abenomics-work.

6 Bank of Japan, 'Outlook for Economic Activity and Prices', 28 April 2021, p. 14, https://www.boj.or.jp/en/mopo/outlook/gor2104b.pdf.

7 Prime Minister's Office of Japan, 'Ichi Oku Sō Katsuyaku Shakai no Jitsugen' [Successful Realisation of a Society of 100 Million], 16 October 2015, https://kantei.go.jp/jp/headline/ichiokusokatsuyaku/index.html.

8 Japan, Cabinet Secretariat, 'Speech on Growth Strategy by Prime Minister Shinzo Abe at the Japan National Press Club', 19 April 2013, https://japan.kantei.go.jp/96_abe/statement/201304/19speech_e.html.

9 Female labour force participation data is taken from the World Bank's database: https://data.

worldbank.org/indicator/SL.TLF.ACTI.FE.ZS?locations=JP. See also Daichi Mishima, 'Japan Sees Record Number of Women Working, but Challenges Remain', *Nikkei Asia*, 30 July 2019, https://asia.nikkei.com/Economy/Japan-sees-record-number-of-women-working-but-challenges-remain.

10 Japan's fertility rate remained far below 1.5 throughout Abe's second premiership, well under the 2.1 replacement rate. OECD, 'Fertility Rates', https://data.oecd.org/pop/fertility-rates.htm.

11 'In Major Shift, Japan Looks to Allow More Foreign Workers to Stay Indefinitely', *Japan Times*, 18 November 2021, https://www.japantimes.co.jp/news/2021/11/18/national/japan-indefinite-visas/.

12 Japan, National Institute of Population and Social Security Research, 'Population Statistics of Japan 2017', 2017, https://www.ipss.go.jp/p-info/e/psj2017/PSJ2017.asp.

13 Inkster, *The Great Decoupling*, p. 193.

14 See Julia Lovell, *Maoism: A Global History* (London: Bodley Head, 2019), pp. 1–24 for a detailed discussion on China's international political activism during the Mao years.

15 'China's Armed Forces: "Informatisation" and "Intelligentisaton"', *The Military Balance 2020* (Abingdon: Routledge for the IISS, 2020), pp. 9–12.

16 Robert Ward, 'RCEP Trade Deal: A Geopolitical Win for China', International Institute for Strategic Studies, 25 November 2020, https://www.iiss.org/blogs/analysis/2020/11/rcep-trade-deal.

17 'New Japan PM Kishida Skeptical China Will Qualify to Join CPTPP', *Nikkei Asia*, 5 October 2021, https://asia.nikkei.com/Politics/New-Japan-PM-Kishida-skeptical-China-will-qualify-to-join-CPTPP.

18 Drew Thompson, 'US–China Decoupling and Its Regional Security Implications', *Asia-Pacific Regional Security Assessment 2021: Key Developments and Trends* (Abingdon: Routledge for the IISS, 2021), p. 14.

19 Hughes, *Japan's Remilitarisation*, p. 145.

20 Abe, *Utsukushii Kuni E* [Towards a Beautiful Country], p. 29. 'Masa ni kempō no kaisei koso ga "dokuritsu no kaifuku" ga shōchō de ari'; see also pp. 123–44.

21 Thompson, 'US–China Decoupling and Its Regional Security Implications', p. 17.

22 Kai Lin Tay, 'China's Military Looks to Civilians to Boost Innovation', International Institute for Strategic Studies, 7 May 2020, https://www.iiss.org/blogs/analysis/2020/05/china-civil-military-innovation.

23 Ward, 'Japan's Security Policy and China', pp. 34–5. See also 'Cyber Capabilities and National Power: A Net Assessment', International Institute for Strategic Studies, 28 June 2021, pp. 79–88 for a detailed discussion of Japan's cyber power in a comparative context.

24 Japan, Ministry of Defense, 'Defense of Japan', 2021, https://www.mod.go.jp/en/publ/w_paper/wp2021/DOJ2021_Digest_EN.pdf.

25 Mitsuru Obe, 'Decoupling Denied: Japan Inc Lays Its Bets on China', *Financial Times*, 16 February 2021, https://www.ft.com/content/d1e2f806-1958-4cd6-8047-e27901786f26.

26 'Nihon no jidōsha kogyō 2020' [Japan's Automobile Industry 2020], Japan Automobile Manufacturers Association, August 2020, p. 5.

27 Ben Dooley and Hisako Ueno, 'Why Japan Is Holding Back as the World Rushes Toward Electric Cars', *New York Times*, 9 March 2021, https://www.nytimes.com/2021/03/09/business/electric-cars-japan.html.

28 Interview with Dr Funabashi Yoichi, Chairman, Asia Pacific Initiative, July 2021.

29 Ayumi Shintaku, 'TSMC to Open Semiconductor R&D Facility in Tsukuba', *Asahi Shimbun*, 1 June 2021, https://www.asahi.com/ajw/articles/14362890.

30 'TSMC Eyes Building Japan Plant in 2022, Start of Operations in 2024', *Kyodo News*, 14 October 2021, https://english.kyodonews.net/news/2021/10/9bc53309be17-breaking-news-tsmc-eyes-building-japan-plant-in-2022-start-of-operations-in-24.html.

31 Amari Akira, '"Senryakuteki Jiritsusei" to "Senryakuteki Fukaketsusei" no Kakuritsu wa Kyūmu' [The Urgency of Securing 'Strategic Autonomy' and 'Strategic Indispensability'], *Gaiko Web*, vol. 68, July/August 2021, http://www.gaiko-web.jp/test/wp-content/uploads/2021/07/Vol68_p6-11_cover_story_interview.pdf.

32 Kana Inagaki and Leo Lewis, 'Japan's Economic Security Minister Warns on Chip Industry Survival', *Financial Times*, 19 October 2021, https://www.ft.com/content/f59173b6-211c-4446-aa57-5c9b78d602c2.

33 Robert Ward, 'Japan's Long-term Foreign Policy: Building Resilience', *Japan Times*, 16 June 2020, https://www.japantimes.co.jp/opinion/2020/06/16/commentary/japan-commentary/japans-long-term-foreign-policy-building-resilience/.

34 Douglas Miller, *You Can't Do Business with Hitler* (London: Hutchinson, 1941). Quoted in Hirschman, *National Power and the Structure of Foreign Trade*, p. 78.

35 OECD, 'Real GDP Long-term Forecast', https://data.oecd.org/gdp/gdp-long-term-forecast.htm.

INDEX

E

East China Sea 16, 45, 50, 55
Economic Planning Agency 32
economic security 12, 14, 25, 28, 35, 49, 51, 59,
    60, 61, 63, 84, 89, 98, 99, 101, 106, 107, 113,
    118, 127, 128, 129
European Union 47, 60, 76, 98, 99, 121

F

Financial Services Agency 107
5G 51, 52, 53, 60, 89, 90, 91, 98, 111, 117
France 16, 17, 19, 37, 40
Free and Open Indo-Pacific 25, 54, 55, 56, 57,
    58, 63, 92, 93, 94, 97, 98, 100, 121
free-trade agreement 77, 95, 96, 97, 127
Fujitsu 42
Fukuda Doctrine 37, 38, 71, 75, 109
Fukuda Takeo 37, 38, 39, 59, 65, 75, 118

G

General Agreement on Tariffs and Trade 33
General Security of Military Information 122
Germany 11, 16, 19, 33, 37, 40, 93
Ground Self-Defense Force 22
G2 50, 51
G5 40, 79, 80
G7 17, 26, 58, 79, 80
G20 25, 58, 60, 80, 98, 99
Guidelines for Japan–US Defense Cooperation
    21, 88
Gulf War 21, 22, 42, 43

H

Hashimoto Ryutaro 21, 22, 23, 67, 82, 107
Hirschman, Albert O. 11, 129
Hong Kong 76
Huawei 52, 53, 91, 98, 118
Hughes, Christopher W. 125

I

Ikeda Hayato 34
India 17, 26, 30, 46–47, 49, 55, 56, 80, 93, 97, 99,
    100, 130
Indonesia 17, 49, 71, 75, 100
Inoki Masamichi 39
International Development Association 33
International Monetary Fund 17, 32, 77, 78, 95
Internet of Things 52

J

Japan Aerospace Exploration Agency 54
Japan Defense Agency 115
Japanese Foreign Exchange and Foreign Trade
    Act 90
Japan–EU Economic Partnership Agreement
    99, 121
Japan–India Global Partnership 47
Japan–US Alliance 88
Japan–US Security Treaty 19, 38, 57
Johnson, Chalmers 108

K

Kishida Fumio 27, 129
Kobayashi Takayuki 129
Koizumi Junichiro 22, 23, 26, 45, 68, 80, 104,
    108, 127
Kosaka Masataka 18, 39, 93, 104, 105
Kuwait 22, 43

L

Liberal Democratic Party 20, 21, 22, 38, 39, 45,
    52, 89, 110, 117
Line (social-media service) 111
Luttwak, Edward N. 12

M

Maritime Self-Defense Force 22
Microsoft 111
Middle East 36, 42, 49, 87
Ministerial Conference for the Economic
    Development of Southeast Asia 34, 38
Ministry of Defense 62, 63, 91, 92, 108, 113, 115,
    116, 127
Ministry of Economy, Trade and Industry 61,
    62, 90, 107, 108, 110
Ministry of Education, Culture, Sports, Science
    and Technology 62
Ministry of Finance 107
Ministry of Foreign Affairs 33, 107
Ministry of Internal Affairs and
    Communications 107
Ministry of International Trade and Industry
    108, 109, 110
Ministry of Land, Infrastructure, Transport and
    Tourism 107
Mitsubishi Electric 54
Miyazawa Kiichi 39

N

Nakasone Yasuhiro 20, 21, 38, 67, 73, 85
National Defense Program Guidelines 23, 62,
    63, 116
National Institute of Population and Social
    Security Research 124
National Intelligence Law 52, 60
National Police Agency 87
National Security Council 84–85, 86, 87, 108, 122
National Security Secretariat 25, 63, 84, 86, 89,
    96, 111, 122
National Security Strategy 57, 62, 84
National Security Technology Research
    Promotion Fund 91
NATO 19, 69, 92
Nine-minister Meeting 85, 86
Nixon, Richard 35, 36, 57
Nokia 52
North Atlantic Council 92
North Atlantic Free Trade Agreement 76
Northern Territories/Kurile Islands 59, 80, 122
Nye, Joseph S. 11
North Korea 21, 76, 106

Adelphi books are published six times a year by Routledge Journals, an imprint of Taylor & Francis, 4 Park Square, Milton Park, Abingdon, Oxfordshire OX14 4RN, UK.

A subscription to the institution print edition, ISSN 1944-5571, includes free access for any number of concurrent users across a local area network to the online edition, ISSN 1944-558X. Taylor & Francis has a flexible approach to subscriptions enabling us to match individual libraries' requirements. This journal is available via a traditional institutional subscription (either print with free online access, or online-only at a discount) or as part of our libraries, subject collections or archives. For more information on our sales packages please visit www.tandfonline.com/page/librarians.

2022 Annual Adelphi Subscription Rates			
Institution	£922	US$1,705	€1,364
Individual	£316	US$541	€433
Online only	£784	US$1,449	€1,159

Dollar rates apply to subscribers outside Europe. Euro rates apply to all subscribers in Europe except the UK and the Republic of Ireland where the pound sterling price applies. All subscriptions are payable in advance and all rates include postage. Journals are sent by air to the USA, Canada, Mexico, India, Japan and Australasia. Subscriptions are entered on an annual basis, i.e. January to December. Payment may be made by sterling cheque, dollar cheque, international money order, National Giro, or credit card (Amex, Visa, Mastercard).

For a complete and up-to-date guide to Taylor & Francis journals and books publishing programmes, and details of advertising in our journals, visit our website: http://www.tandfonline.com.

Ordering information:
USA/Canada: Taylor & Francis Inc., Journals Department, 530 Walnut Street, Suite 850, Philadelphia, PA 19106, USA. **UK/Europe/Rest of World:** Routledge Journals, T&F Customer Services, T&F Informa UK Ltd., Sheepen Place, Colchester, Essex, CO3 3LP, UK.

Advertising enquiries to:
USA/Canada: The Advertising Manager, Taylor & Francis Inc., 530 Walnut Street, Suite 850, Philadelphia, PA 19106, USA. Tel: +1 (800) 354 1420. Fax: +1 (215) 207 0050. **UK/Europe/Rest of World**: The Advertising Manager, Routledge Journals, Taylor & Francis, 4 Park Square, Milton Park, Abingdon, Oxfordshire OX14 4RN, UK. Tel: +44 (0) 20 7017 6000. Fax: +44 (0) 20 7017 6336.